THE
SECRET PLACES
OF
THE BURREN

JOHN M. FEEHAN

The mass of men live lives of quiet desperation.

R_CB
ROYAL CARBERY BOOKS

ROYAL CARBERY BOOKS
36 Beechwood Park, Ballinlough, Cork

Trade Distributors:
Mercier Press
PO Box 5, 5 French Church Street, Cork
16 Hume Street, Dublin 2

ISBN 0 946645 05 1

13 12 11 10 9 8 7 6 5 4

Acknowledgements

I would like to thank the following who helped me with this book.
Naturally the opinions expressed here are mine and not necessarily
theirs: Chris O'Neill of O'Neill's Town House Lisdoonvarna where I
stay when I am in the Burren; Micheál Vaughan of the Aberdeen Arms
Hotel, Lahinch, Naoise O'Clery, Mary & Frankie O'Gorman, Seán
Spellessy, James Healy, Cathleen Cullen, Bernie Power, Mary McGrath,
Mary O'Brien, and the staff of the Clare County Library particularly
Noel Crowley and Mary Moroney. A special word of thanks to Hilary
Richardson who drew the illustrations. Go mba fada buan iad go léir.
                                                                    J.M.F.

Printed in Ireland by Colour Books Ltd,

CONTENTS

DEDICATED TO
THE MEMORY OF
MARY P. KISSANE
AND THOSE LOVELY SUMMER DAYS
IN THE VALLEY OF THE FERTILE ROCK

INTRODUCTION

Love had he found in huts where poor men lie;
His daily teachers had been woods and hills,
The silence that is in the starry sky,
The sleep that is among the lonely hills.

WORDSWORTH

Many years ago I wrote three successful travel books and I followed them in recent years by four even more successful political books. Now I am back again to travel writing which is my first love.

It is great to be out in the fresh open air exploring the little hidden corners of Ireland instead of trying to explore the caverns of men's minds. This book, I must emphasise, is not a guide book. There are two excellent guide books to the Burren written by George Cunningham, *Burren Journey* and *Burren Journey West* and I understand he has written a third which will be published in the near future. These books, as well as the Burren map by T.D. Robinson and the Ballyvaughan map by Ann Korff and Jeff O'Connell are an essential help to an understanding of this present book. I hope you have wisely bought them – they are indispensable to the traveller in the Burren.

9

I wrote most of these pages on different visits to the Burren and as the pattern of my life began to change. There is no doubt youth is a fine thing but serenity comes with age – and serenity is the foyer to happiness. Youth begets pleasure which is short-lived and fleeting. Age begets joy which is more lasting and more fulfilling. 'All my life I sought pleasure and pleasure is so sad,' lamented Oscar Wilde. I suppose the transition came for me when I began to *experience* places and things rather than just *seeing* them as a tourist and exclaiming – 'Wonderful! Let's go!' I am afraid I was one of those tourists who travelled to satisfy my vanity and not my heart. I was part of a society for whom the real beauties of nature were invisible and whose conversation rarely rose beyond the enumeration of those people of importance seen in a day.

This experiencing of things, rather than just seeing them, came about as a result of my interest in alternative styles of living which have startled the world in the last twenty years. It is as if we humans are entering a new stage of evolution – the exploration of a spiritual dimension composed of some form of energy as yet not fully understood. Although there has been some slight awakening in Ireland, we are still very backward in our awareness of world thought. Dr D. H. Andrews, Professor of Chemistry at Johns Hopkins University said: 'It is not seeing with the eye but seeing with the mind that gives us a basis for belief, and in this way science and religion are one.' I had seen the Burren again and again. It was only when I began to experience it, to feel the atmosphere, the mystery, the peace, the character, that it slowly started to speak to me and reveal tiny fragments of its store of secrets. What I have written here is the result of this veiled interchange of mystical thought, or, if you like, unknown energy. There is so much completely hidden from us – so much that we cannot understand, so many unwritten chapters.

The more I got to know the Burren the more suspicious I became of 'expert' opinion. Many times I found myself face to face with the simple truth of the fact that we know hardly anything of pre-Christian Ireland. Most of what the scholars tell us about those far-off days is mere guess-work. But there is nothing wrong with guess-work provided it is clearly seen to be such. It is when dogmatic statements purporting to be the truth are made, when all they are is pure speculation, that confidence is shattered. So I would advise my readers to exercise extreme caution before accepting much of what is written about pre-Christian and indeed early Christian Ireland. Use your own common sense, relax and try to become one with the past and maybe it will let slip a few of its many secrets. That great Cambridge scholar, Kathleen Hughes, wrote:

. . For instance, historical sources tell us very little indeed about the limestone plateau of the Burren in northern County Clare. It is today empty and silent, yet if you go there alone the awareness of man's past presses upon you with an almost frightening urgency, for wherever you turn your head there are signs of the human past from dolmens to forts, ancient fields and churches.

The Burren is not a kind of Rubicube to be solved but an intriguing mystery to be enjoyed.

A few readers of my other travel books suggested that much of what I write is anti-British. That is really an unfair comment. I am certainly anti-tyranny, whether such tyranny comes from German, Russian, British or American sources, but I am not anti-British as such. Tyranny is viciously evil no matter what uniform enforces it. The harsh reality is that it was the British, not the Nazis or the Russians, who sent millions of our people to their death, sold hundreds of thousands of others into slavery, and turned our country into one enormous death-camp.

In the 1960s in Ireland, as well as the hula-hoop, sideburns, long hair and narrow trousers, there came upon the scene another fad which was destined to carry itself over to the present day but like all fads is now fading rapidly. This fad came to be known as 'revisionist history'. The main theme of this bubble was that we all mis-understood Irish history. The British were not our enemies. They were actually acting in our best interests but we did not appreciate it. All round we should be grateful to the British for the considerate care they showered upon us during the Famine and the Black-and-Tan regime. De Valera, Pádraig Pearse, Michael Collins and Terence MacSwiney, were all evil subversives who deserved what-ever punishment they got. Shakespeare probably put the best description of some of these revisionists into the mouth of Iago:

> . . . duteous and knee-crooking knave
> that doting on his own obsequious bondage
> weans out his time much like his master's ass
> for nought but provender.

The fact that I told the harsh and bitter truth in my books annoyed many of these 'jackdaws in peacocks feathers'. I offer them no apology. They will find the same truths in this book. I simply cannot turn history around. However, I must make a clear distinction between the British Estab-lishment, who were responsible for the evil, and the British people who were quite innocent and did not know what was being done in their name. From the heights of their armour-plated arrogance this Establishment despised everyone, English or Irish, outside their class. The ordinary British tourists who come in thousands to this country every year have been kept in almost complete ignorance of what really happened, and my experience is that they are most anxious to search out the truth. This surely explains the enormous sales of books in Irish tourist outlets to British visitors, which expose this, and especially books on the Six Counties. The majority of these tourists, far from being offended, experience a deep sorrow that any of their rulers could have been so heartless and cruel, and they have made a common bond with the Irish people who have responded by welcoming them. The best homage we ourselves can pay our brave ancestors is to try to make the Ireland they handed over to us at such gigantic sacrifice a better place for everyone to live in and to do this without rancour or bitterness towards anyone, especially towards the British people.

Readers of my previous travel books will remember Maxie, my Alsatian-Husky dog. He accompanied me on most of my trips in the Burren and it was a sheer delight to be with him. I needed no other companion. Sadly, old age has been creeping up on him and for the last year or so he is no longer able to walk for more than ten or fifteen minutes at a time. Maxie has always been welcome where-ever I go, in pubs, hotels and even in retreat houses. When I made retreats of spiritual renewal in monasteries and con-vents he was accepted, fed and looked after. The only exception to these acts of kindness happened, I am sorry to say, in the Burren. I was attending a talk in the lecture hall of the Convent of Mercy in Lisdoonvarna and I had with me Misty, a small cairn terrier, spotlessly clean and house-trained. When I tried to bring him in to the lecture hall I was stopped by a nun who informed me in clear terms that she could not allow him in. No amount of pleading moved her, not even an appeal to the spirit of St Francis, the animals' friend, and I was forced to bring the little creature back to the car and leave him there in the melting heat of the sun. It seemed to me that this act contrasted strangely with the spiritual maxims which adorned the walls of the convent at various places, one of which showed a child with young birds and the caption: 'Stand still and consider the wondrous works of God'. I presume a small helpless dog is also one of the wondrous works of God. Contrasting strangely with these maxims too was the graffiti scribbled on the backs of the chairs in the lecture hall – graffiti which was vulgar, tasteless and not even funny. I recalled a notice about dogs which I once saw in a hotel:

Of course your dog is welcome. In our long experience of the hotel business no dog has ever stolen our linen and towels, no dog has broken our glasses in a drunken brawl, no dog has ever tried to seduce our female staff, no dog has ever passed a dud cheque on us. If you can guarantee yourself to be as well behaved as your dog, you too are welcome.

They might have added:

No dog has ever written filthy graffiti on our furniture – that was left to our human visitors.

Unfortunately in this book I have only been able to touch on a mere fragment of the Burren. To cover it properly one would almost need to compile an encyclopaedia. However, this limitation may well have an advantage. It may encourage you to do a bit of exploration for yourself. For example a lot of the south-eastern area of the Burren has been scantily explored. Only the great fort at Cahercommaun has been fully excavated and this yielded one extraordinary mystery. Human bones were found in a garbage heap – but they were chopped up as if they had been part of a stew served for dinner. Were we once cannibals?

The area enclosed between Kilnaboy, Boston, Carron and Leamaneagh is teeming with interest and includes the Seven Streams of Teeskagh, which pour out of seven openings in a cliff and are reputed to be an infallible cure for impotence. I do not know whether you drink the waters or apply them to the affected parts. No doubt if you make a discreet enquiry locally you will find out. This area abounds in secret places, legends, stories and mysteries. So arm yourself with maps and guide books and venture into the unknown. Who knows what you might find? For the present, however, come along with me through the pages of this book and I will introduce you to some of the secret places of the Burren. You may not find any great material treasure but I think you will find something much more valuable – that elusive peace which a thousand inner voices promised in the past. You may well shake off the burden of the years, the formulas by which life must be lived, the appearances to be kept up, the daily mask which must be worn. Much of the sadnesses, stresses and frustrations can vanish into the vibrating life of beauty around you and you may well be able to make your own of the words of that gifted poet, William Blake:

> I see a world in a grain of sand
> And a heaven in a wild flower;
> Hold infinity in the palm of your hand
> And eternity in an hour.

One thing, however, is certain: you will never forget your friendship with the Burren.

J.M.F.
February 1987

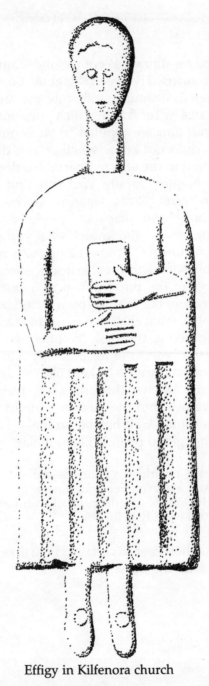

Effigy in Kilfenora church

ONE

LAND OF MYSTERY – LAND OF THE FREE

And therefore, Burren hills, grey Burren hills,
Soul of fierce Clare, wild west of all our west,
No mindless tract of earth or strand thou seemst
Such as dull maps and solemn charts attest,
Here 'mid your solitudes as 'mid the crowds
Alike for me thou shinest, realm apart;
Open to all we pine for, pray for, hope;
Sanctified homeland of the unchanging heart.

EMILY LAWLESS

When people read tourist literature or hear someone talking about a holiday in the Burren, the question they most frequently ask is, 'What is the Burren?' The name does not conjure up any specific image except perhaps to the Irish scholar who knows that the word itself means 'a rocky place'. And the Burren is surely one of the rockiest places in all of Europe.

The Burren is a part of north-west County Clare bounded on the north and west by the Atlantic Ocean and on the south and east by an invisible line roughly from Doolin to

Kilfenora to New Quay on the shores of Galway bay. At first glance it is almost scarey with its austere, bewildering landscape and geometric rock formations so unlike the wild disordered boulders scattered with such abandon in other beauty spots of Ireland.

This, of course, is only a first impression – an impression which vanishes immediately one explores at close quarters its inviting panorama. For the Burren is vibrating with life and every new vista holds out promise of:

> A presence that disturbs me with the joy
> Of elevated thoughts; a sense sublime
> Of something far more deeply interfused
> Whose dwelling is the light of setting suns
> And the round ocean and the living air
> And the blue sky, and in the mind of man.

One of the fascinations of the Burren is that it stands out in such remarkable contrast to the rest of Ireland which the tourist literature describes as a land of mists and bogs, lush green pastures, enchanting mountains and shimmering lakes. It is as if the dream of a god wantonly pitchforked a gem of severe classical beauty into our midst, and scattered some kind of fallen star dust over the earth. Nowhere else in Ireland can one find those eerie white-terraced mountains which sometimes exude such strange lights: a steely blue in the early morning which by mid-day casts shadows of purple, blending into an evening gold and turning to a frightening dark grey as night closes in. It is a land of terraced mountains, sunken valleys, hidden caves, exotic flowers and scattered everywhere are the relics of our stormy past. The Burren has remained aloof from the rest of Ireland as if it wanted to jealously guard its mysteries which have baffled so many who were foolish enough to presume they could solve them.

For the first words the Burren speaks to us are words of mystery. Words which challenge us to wrest from this time-less landscape the secrets of its soul. Perhaps the most closely guarded secret of all is: How did it happen? How did it come about? It is as well to begin by admitting the truth which is, that we do not know.

The scholars tell us that millions of years ago a moving glacier in which massive boulders were embedded sud-denly stopped and melted, depositing rocks in North Clare. Why it should stop so suddenly and proceed to melt is not fully explained. Neither is it explained where the rocks came from or how come some of the rocks were hard type, namurian, and others soft type, limestone, or how these different types of rocks fitted themselves neatly into various parts of the Burren as if the ground had been made ready for them. But this is mostly theory based on tenuous evidence. The truth is that we really do not know. It all happened so long ago and none of us were around at the time.

There is however another theory, equally credible, which I heard in a Lisdoonvarna pub late one night when the ale was flowing freely and the merriment was at its highest. It was expounded in the form of a learned discourse by a jovial travelling tinker with a roguish pair of eyes and lines of devilment escaping from the corners of his smiling mouth.

"Tis this way it happened,' he said, gazing solemnly at the British tourists but at the same time managing a surrep-titious wink at the rest of the company in the bar. "Tis how the man in the moon and his wife got blind drunk one St Patrick's Day and had the father-and-mother of a row. They belted one another 'round the moon and knocked sparks off the rocks which turned into the stars you see on a bright winter's night. Anyway the missus was getting the worst of the fight and she ran away hell-for-leather as fast as her feet could carry her. Himself took after her with a big sledge-hammer and she ran in behind a cluster of rocks. He was in such a temper that he drew a belt at her with the hammer shouting "burren" which is moon language for an unmentionable four letter word. She was quick enough for him and she ducked. He hit the rock an almightly blow, cracked it and away it went into space with the missus hanging on to it and kept flying through the air collecting other rocks until it landed here in Clare. When the locals heard all the commotion they gathered round the queer looking woman who was lying the full length of the half-mile strand in Fanore. All of a sudden she opened her eyes, looked at the crowd around her and screamed "burren", and dropped dead on the spot. They gave her a decent wake and funeral with candles and snuff, there and then, and covered her with tons of sand, which became the sand hill you can see today. That's how it all began and how the Burren got its name. I'm tellin' ye no word of a lie.'

No doubt this version earned the tinker several pints from the bewildered British tourists but is his version less credible than the glacier theory? An intelligent academic, anxious to impress his peers, could very easily collect enough circumstantial evidence to prove this folk tale worthy of belief.

There is, however, some slight evidence to show that the Burren was not always the wild rocky place it is today. There is a possibility that it was once covered with soil and trees. Woodland snails dating to 3000 BC can yet be found in the Burren and some excavations have unearthed stumps of trees going back a thousand years. What happened? In the sixteenth and seventeenth centuries the British occupation forces cleared most of the trees in Ireland to prevent the Irish guerrilla bands from finding cover. If this happened in the Burren then the weather would have eroded the soil and exposed the bare rock underneath. 'What shall we do for timber, the best of the woodland is gone,' mourned the poet of Kilcash who might well have been mourning the Burren.

Another of the Burren's well kept secrets is the origin and behaviour of its exotic flora. In the crevices between the rocks some of the world's most beautiful and scarcest flowers can be found, blooming all on their own without help of any kind from man. There are many unusual features about the Burren flora not found elsewhere in Europe. Rare Alpine flowers grow side by side with Mediterranean flowers. Lime-hating flowers grow side by side with lime-loving flowers. Sea shore flora can be found on hill tops and hill top flora grows near the sea shore.

Many theories have been put forward but again they are only theories. The high density of light from the sea and the rock is said to help this growth as is also the natural warmth of the rock which acts as a kind of storage heater and retains the heat during the winter. There is no doubt but that these conditions affect growth advantageously but it does not explain fully the presence side by side of flora so ecologically different. It is as if some great unseen power, that we know not of as yet, has infused all these varying beauties into the world of the Burren. But the mystery remains. It holds its secret still.

Where did all this rare flora come from? Again the scholars theory is that the ice brought one type of flower seed, the Alpine, with it, and the other, the Mediterranean type, was already there. That theory I find a little difficult to accept. The tinker in the Lisdoonvarna pub had a different theory. After the sixth pint he confided to the tourists that the night they waked the man-in-the-moon's wife they found a packet of mixed flower-seed hidden in her knickers.

Large cross in Kilfenora graveyard, detail of south side

She was such a big woman that the packet weighed nearly a half-hundred weight and it took two strong men to lift it. They left the seed on top of her grave and that night the fairies, under the leadership of one, Johnny McGlory, took it away and scattered it all over the landscape. These are two view – so take your choice.

Yet another theory as to where the seed came from was advanced to me by a mountainy farmer – an intelligent well-read man, whose life was spent shepherding his flock and who knew intimately most of the outstanding features of the Burren. His words had a ring of timelessness about them. He believed that, not only in pre-Christian times but also in early Christian Ireland, there were constant and regular comings and goings between the Burren and the continent of Europe. Many of these travellers and pilgrims brought back seed with them which they planted, and then nature simply took its course and over the centuries the seeds were scattered by winds and birds all over the landscape. This theory cannot be lightly dismissed because there is considerable evidence, particularly at monastic sites, of the existence of well cultivated and extensive terraced gardens. The natural inclination of those monastic gardeners would be to have as many plants as possible in their gardens. But while this may well explain the existence of the flora it does not explain their mysterious growth habits.

The mystery remains and each year scores of botany specialists visit the Burren but as yet no one has found a completely satisfactory answer.

In 1839 John O'Donovan, the great Irish antiquarian, wrote:

I returned yesterday evening from the wild rocks of the Burren where I was hurt by a mule but not very severely. Burren is the wildest and ruggedest district I have yet seen and I found it exceedingly difficult to cross the single limestone with which it abounds. . . I have met several ancient churches in the primitive Irish style and in beautiful preservation. . . perfect specimens of the earliest architecture of Christian times in Ireland.

Not only has the Burren more than its share of these ancient ruins but there is also a profusion of pre-Christian archaeological remains. Per square mile they are amongst the most numerous in Europe. All kinds of explanations have been put forward as to what these things actually are and why there should be so many, but the enigma still remains.

Most of these theories have been put forward by archae-ologists but while these people have a certain technical competence such as a knowledge of methods of dating etc., they have by no means a monopoly on commonsense, and few, if any, are trained in anthropology. Like garage mechanics who are competent in technical matters, but not expert in driving, these learned people should be regarded as good technicians. It would therefore be unfair to expect them to answer many of the questions the Burren poses. It would not, however, be unfair to criticise them severely for putting forward wild outlandish theories instead of being simple and straightforward enough to say, 'I just don't know'. The technical information they can give is valuable. The interpretation of that technical knowledge should be left to others.

One of the theories put forward by some suggests that pre-historic man found the Burren an attractive and suitable place to settle down and live in. This theory, however, is not too easy to understand. Why should people choose a barren, windswept countryside to make their homes and

rear their families when there was so much rich, fertile land in abundance elsewhere? One can understand that a number of exceptional people might like to live in beauty and isolation but hardly the masses of ordinary men, women and children. Herein, I think, lies a clue.

In every religion, and especially in early Irish Christianity, there were always the select groups who felt a call to a close and intimate union with God beyond the norms of ordinary ethical living. To achieve this union and to live a life of absolute asceticism they moved away from the centres of population and took up their abode in isolated off-beat areas which were also areas of great beauty. The whole history of early religion teems with examples of this kind of movement towards solitude.

Now, if the Christian religions could inspire such movements amongst its followers, surely it is reasonable to assume that the old pagan religions could do likewise. Is there any reason why sections of pre-Christian Ireland should not feel a call to higher things and band themselves into small isolated communities for worship and prayer? The early Christians sought union with God as the source of life. Could not the early Irish pagans have sought union with their source of life, the sun, which they worshipped? Where better could they worship the sun than in the Burren where the rocky landscape attracts its rays like a magnet and indeed stores them for long periods.

The distinguished philosopher Rudolf Steiner wrote:

The inner qualities of the Sun factor, how these permeate the earth and how they are again radiated back from the earth into cosmic space – this was what the druid priest was able to see in the dolmens. The physical nature of the light of the sun was warded off, a dark space was created by the stones, which were set in the soil with a roof stone above them, and in this dark shadowed space it was possible by seeing through the rocks the spiritual nature and being of the sunlight.

From this it might be inferred that the Burren was a holy place, a place of contemplation and prayer, like the Egyptian desert, and that it was primarily peopled for this reason rather than for material reasons.

Of course the short answer to all this again is that we simply do not know. But there is at least a *prima facie* case for supposing that in the past the Burren was seen as a place of holiness, a place close to God, a place of retreat where people striving for higher things found inspiration and help. If we see the Burren in that light then we may have to adjust some theories about many of its archaeological remains, but we may well come closer to understanding its mysteries.

Two particular types of monuments of the pre-Christian era are found in the Burren: portal monuments and wedge monuments. The general view put forward is that these were tombs of some kind. But were they? There is some evidence to suggest that people were buried there but the intriguing question is: were they built as tombs in the first place? Within the precincts of Kilfenora and Corcomroe churches there are several graves, but these places were not originally built as tombs.

It was, and indeed is, a common religious superstition that if one is buried within the precincts of a church or sacred place one stands a better chance of getting into heaven. This of course is sheer theological nonsense; God is not a county council chairman who can be squared, or impressed by a man's last resting place. The king and the tinker look exactly alike a few months after death. Nevertheless it is a very human sort of a superstition. An old Irish proverb says: *Is fearr focal sa chúirt na púnt sa sparán.* (A friendly word in the right place is better than money in the purse). This human view may well explain the burials under some of these monuments. The fact that people were buried there does not mean that they were originally built as tombs. In Wales, for example, these monuments are referred to as 'Druids' Altars' not tombs. Also in Kilmogue the monument there is called Leac an Scáil – The Stone of the Shadow – which might easily suggest an astrological explanation.

Again we simply do not know what these monuments were for. If we accept the possibility that the Burren was regarded as a holy place then the presence of these monuments opens up many engaging possibilities and we certainly cannot rule out an astrological dimension.

Martin Brennan in his book *The Stars and the Stones* opens up amazing new lines of enquiry into Ireland's megalithic monuments. He sees them as intimately connected with astronomy, with the positions of the sun at different times of the year and suggests that true sundials and calendar stones were a significant feature of ancient Ireland. Although he is primarily concerned with megalithic art I sincerely hope that he would some day give us a book on the Burren and bring fresh new scholarly thinking to that intriguing area.

If we follow this line of thought we must naturally ask: if they were not primarily burial places what were they? This question is being asked about thousands of other ancient monuments in all parts of the world. Let us divert for a moment and look at one, the Great Pyramid of Egypt on the Giza plain.

This magnificent monument presents us with the same enigma. Again the reality is that nobody really knows what it was for or even how it was built. The experts tell us that it was a tomb of the Pharaohs, but have produced no evidence. No body of a Pharaoh has even been found in the Great Pyramid. In fact there is no evidence that it was a burial place at all. But early in this century an unusual thing happened. An intelligent French tourist named Andre Bovis noticed, while visiting the pyramid, some dead animals and some discarded food which should have been rotting and smelly but were not. When he exmined them closely he came to the conclusion that the dead animals and the food were mummified. This astounded him and he began to wonder if the Pyramid generated an energy unknown to present-day man but known to the ancient Egyptians.

When Bovis returned to France he built a small timber Pyramid to the exact scaled-down measurement of the Great Pyramid. He experimented with meat and fruit and found that it did not rot but mummified. So it seemed there was after all a strange energy working. The experts, however, did not accept his findings, but Bovis persevered, and today some of the world's top scientists accept the presence of a strange unknown energy in Pyramid forms. Both Nobel prizewinner Wolfgang Pauli and Swiss psychologist Carl Jung suggest that there definitely is another force operating in the world – a force we know very little about.

It is not within the scope of this book to discuss in detail this strange energy but for those interested I can suggest two very good books, *Pyramid Energy Handbook* by Serge V. King, Ph.D. and *The Psychic Power of Pyramids* by Bill Schul and Ed Pettit.

Recent research and experimentation has discovered another curious thing about pyramids: those who are ill and sit in their own home-made ones have experienced certain cures. A kind of a feeling of aloneness, not an unpleasant type, comes over some people. Others experience an extraordinary feeling of security and safety. Those who practice meditation have found that if they meditate inside a pyramid they feel a very much heightened sense of being and a strange awareness of the actual energy

What is most interesting of all is that it seems a similar energy has been generated inside things like igloos and beehive cells. Was this why such cells were popular with the ancient Irish monks?

All this leads me to pose the question: Could the megalithic monuments have been an Irish version of energy generators? Could they have been places of spiritual healing? Of meditation? Of prayer? Could they be the remains of great monuments to the lost knowledge, culture and spirituality of the Irish race?

Again we do not know the answer to these questions but surely our scholars should be asking them, in conjunction with psychologists, physicists and other experts. Even if these theories seem unusual they are not as outlandish as a lot of theories put forward by archaeologists to date, such as the silly theory that everything they do not understand is a burial place.

One thing, however, we can be sure of and that is how little we know of these things and how inadequate are the explanations offered to us by those to whom we turn for enlightenment.

I believe that the common sense of the average well-read traveller in the Burren might come up with an intelligent and reasonable answer, especially as most of what we have been told to date is mere guess work.

While all these tantalising enigmas float around and attract the attention of enquirers there is yet another feature of the Burren that affords no easy answer. That feature is the character and composition of its people.

There is a particular type of physical beauty that one notices quite often in many who live in or near the Burren which is not found elsewhere in Ireland; dark brown eyes, sallow skin and jet black hair. Some believe that these unusual looks were some kind of a throw-back to the Spanish sailors, survivors of the ill-fated Spanish Armada in 1589 who remained in Clare and intermarried with the Irish. Romantic as this idea may be it is only fanciful thinking. The British saw to it that none of these survivors stayed alive. Although they were prisoners-of-war the troops slaughtered them as they came ashore and only a few escaped. There is no evidence to show that any of them stayed in Clare.

It is more likely that the people of the Burren are pure descendants of the ancient Celts of a thousand years BC. Because of the harsh nature of the landscape the invaders found little here to attract them and so they moved on to more fertile lands to make their settlements. Again the slaughter of the population by the British in the sixteenth, seventeenth and eighteenth centuries which was widespread and thorough in the rest of Ireland, only touched the Burren. Even with the destruction of the woods, the whole nature of the terrain gave so much protection to the Irish that militarily it was not worth the effort and the cost. In this way it seems as if large areas remained virtually undisturbed for thousands of years. This may well explain the physical features of sections of the inhabitants as it may well explain another outstanding characteristic of these people – that is their spirit of independence.

This spirit of independence is probably the most outstanding characteristic of the people of the Burren, a characteristic which is largely absent from the rest of Ireland. However nauseating and unpleasant, we must accept the fact that the slave mind is one of the predominent characteristics of the Irish people. For hundreds of years we have been crawling at the feet of the British and begging a few crumbs from their table. They were the masters and we were forced to tip our forelocks and make obeisance before our betters whenever they came within sight. Today large numbers of the Irish live out that servile role in their daily lives. The British are still their superiors. We are not in the Commonwealth but we are of it. Of this the Nobel Peace Prizewinner, Seán MacBride has this to say:

Every country which has been the subject of foreign domination or colonialism inevitably suffers from some degree of slave mentality. . Many of our politicians, academics and media people have become subserviant to this slave mentality.

Large numbers of the Irish people have come to love their degrading servitude and they remain on their knees still grovelling before their master, still wearing the invisible chains of slavery. One has only to look at the performance of some Irish politicians to realise, with shame, what toadyism really is in Ireland.

The people of the Burren are by and large the exception to these traits. They are not on their knees begging for a spit of recognition. Perhaps this is because the British never really conquered them – landlordism never really got a grip. Whatever the reason is they are certainly not slaves.

For many years I had a holiday cottage in the Burren where, as far as was practicable, I spent the summer months together with my wife, Mary, and our growing children. It was in those glorious far-off days that I came close to the ordinary people and came to appreciate the truth of Montaigne's belief that a landscape can mould the character of those who live there. The rugged solidity of the Burren reflected itself in their whole approach to life. They never forgot that they were Irish through and through. It was at that particular time when yuppyism was being born in Dublin. The yuppies wanted change for the sake of change. The people of the Burren wanted change only if there was a good reason for it. In those heady days when the yuppies deluded themselves into believing that we were a potentially great economic force the Burren man knew that in reality we were only a third world country and they held on to their old ways as long as these ways were effective. When they ceased to be effective, then and only then, they changed.

Their down-to-earth common sense, their integrity, their ability to penetrate a shallow mind, their honesty, were qualities that endeared them to me, qualities unfortunately, I did not come across too often in the rest of Ireland.

One of the unusual hazards which face the people of the Burren is their proneness to broken bones. This happens because of the rocky nature of the farmland which can be dangerous both for human and beast. And so all through its history the services of bonesetters were in constant demand. One of these bonesetters, Thomas Burke, anxious to spare the poor people the expense of setting, hit upon the idea of getting himself elected to parliament, taking his salary but not attending its proceedings and in this way setting the broken bones without having to charge for his services. He managed to get elected and he put his plan into operation with happy and successful results for all sufferers. Burke is long since dead, but he is remembered as a delightful kind man who helped the poor of Clare and who at the same time was not above upbraiding them at election time as this address shows:

I once again appeal to the voters of every shade of politics and religion in Co. Clare, I do so now with mixed feelings. You saw I had a tough time at the last election to get even the fifth seat, though I had given the use of their limbs to people of every class without fee or reward, and I never asked to what party any of them belonged when they came to me. But now when I want their no. 1 votes I have to go on my knees almost to get the votes off them. I do not at all think that treatment fair especially when I thought I had earned their votes and gratitude. It is very disappointing when I find people so ungrateful as to forget what I have done for them when they are no use to themselves or to anybody else only a bundle of shattered bones. Now when they can do their daily work, surely I should expect a simple stroke of a pencil – that is the only compensation I ask. . .

I need hardly tell you that I am sincerely grateful for the votes I get, as a great many vote for me whom I never did a turn for. Hoping you will be true to yourselves and to me by giving me your no. 1 votes.

As ever,
the same old Bonesetter
Thomas Burke

If the Burren is a spiritual place so too are its people. If it is a mysterious place so too are its people. This is wholly consistent with the laws of the universe; that which is spiritual is mysterious and that which is mysterious is spiritual.

I am not alone in my opinion of these people. Writing in 1839 the great Irish scholar, Eugene O'Curry, said that the people here were more historically intelligent 'by one thousand degrees' than the people of the rest of Ireland. All in all they may well be the purest of pure Irish while the rest of us may only be a patchwork of different races.

The Burren then, is not only a place of beauty, but also a place of mystery, peopled by an indestructible race. This combination may well explain why so many intelligent tourists come here – tourists who are searching for something more than a holiday on the sizzling sands or smoke-filled pubs.

TWO

THE FIRST VISTA

O World invisible we view thee
O World intangible we touch thee
O World unknowable we know thee
Inapprehensible we clutch thee
FRANCIS THOMPSON

If you approach the Burren from the south, that is from the Ennis direction, you first meet the picturesque village of Corofin with its old world houses and narrow streets. Corofin is not part of the Burren proper. It is perched on the border-line, like a little ante-chamber, but it is well worth pausing here, not only because of its cosy, merry hostelries but because of the wonderful venture now internationally known as The Clare Heritage Centre. Take a right turn in the village and a few hundred yards in front of you the centre is housed in the old Protestant church in a sylvan setting of character and dignity.

The Clare Heritage Centre is the brain-child of Mr Naoise O'Clery who wanted it to become 'an interpretative museum which would enable visitors to understand more clearly the trauma of nineteenth-century Ireland and the root causes of mass emigration at this period. He hoped also to preserve in a local context many items of historical value, to enlighten and assist persons trace their Clare roots.'

When you stroll around this delightful little museum you cannot help feeling an extraordinary sense of belonging. Memories of the old world of Clare are all around: weapons, flags, paintings, farm implements, household utensils, letters, posters, documents. Tastefuly displayed with love and care they are all in one way or another, an intimate reminder of the tragic and heartbreaking story of the ordinary Irish country folk. Strolling reflectively around this historic centre it is difficult not to be moved by the indomitable spirit of the simple people.

Another great service given by this centre is that it helps people to trace their Clare ancestry. If you have any Clare connections, or any suspected skeleton in the cupboard, the courteous and discreet staff will help you sort them out.

Do not forget to examine the large scale model of a section of the Burren region which shows the strange stone land-scape and the complete limestone drainage system of the area – a model which you would do well to study before a visit to the area.

As you drive out of Corofin the rugged face of the Burren begins to appear. Rocks peep through the multi-coloured earth as if they were popping their heads up to welcome you and to invite you to share the peace of this living poetry.

A few miles along a winding picturesque road you come to the real beginning of the Burren, Kilnaboy. Kilnaboy got its name from a female Irish saint of long ago: Cill Inghine Baoith, the church of the daughter of Baoith. I doubt if Kilnaboy was a monastery, more likely it was a convent and Inghine Baoith an abbess there. Her name in English became Innerwee and in the last century this name was a favourite one for girls. What a pity it fell into disuse. If I were a girl I would love to be called Innerwee – it has about it a bewitching music, sparkling poetry and roguish vibrations!

It is here in Kilnaboy that we meet the first Burren ruins of very early Christian churches. One of the reasons Christianity took root so quickly in Ireland had to do with the ancient Irish obsession with geneaology. The respect in which a family was held in the community depended greatly on their ancestors. Who the parents, grandparents and great-grandparents were became yardsticks by which their standing was judged. Therefore when Christianity taught them that they were the children of God they were beside themselves with delight and they embraced that role with enthusiasm and joy.

Just before we come to Kilnaboy Church we meet the ruins of Coad Church, built by the notorious Máire Rua of Leamaneagh Castle to spite the parish priest of Kilnaboy, whom she did not like, and which is said to contain the graves of her two daughters.

Once over a pint of ale in a Corofin pub a Kilnaboy man told me the delightful story of how Coad got its name. He explained to me that there once lived in that area a petty king called Teige O'Brien. It was said of Teige, who was a typical playboy, that his week's work was divided as follows: Boozing on Sunday, judgements on Monday, cardplaying on Tuesday, hunting on Wednesday, wife and family Thursday, racing on Friday and fornication on Saturday. Now Teige, who was always up to some mischief, once got himself into very serious trouble with the clergy. My informant would not tell me exactly why, since, as he said, he did not like to speak disrespectfully of the dead. Teige was prevailed upon to go to confession to confess his grave sin (no question of marrying the girl!) and the penance he got was that he should erect a standing stone the same height as himself in honour of the Blessed Virgin. The Irish word for equal length was *comh-fhad*, so he built the standing stone and this was later anglicised to Coad. All that happened before Freud's time and had the distinguished professor known of it, it is more than likely that he would have taken a different view of the standing stone and the monk who gave the extraordinary penance. However the stone is still there near the ruins of Coad Church – a subtle reminder to the Kilnaboy people to behave themselves lest they be given a more severe penance.

The first thing that strikes one about Kilnaboy, having ascended the weather-beaten steps, is the Cross of Lorraine on the gable facing the entrance. Strangely enough there is scant reference to this cross in the guide books and nowhere have I seen an attempted explanation as to how it got there. This cross is not incised or cut into the wall. It is shaped out of the actual building stones themselves. Why should the Cross of Lorraine be here? The cross was originally a symbol indicating the presence of a relic of the True Cross in a building, but there is no tradition that there was ever a relic of the True Cross in Kilnaboy. It was the standard of Joan of Arc, but since Joan was not rehabilitated until the twentieth century it is unlikely she would be honoured in any part of the church before then. It was also the standard of the Crusaders and it may well be that some Kilnaboy nun on the continent saw the standard and had the cross sculpted for her own church in Clare. It was also widely used as a protection against vampires but we have no vampire tradition in Ireland, least of all in Kilnaboy. The truth is we do not know how it got there or what its significance is in that setting.

Another extraordinary thing about Kilnaboy is the Sheila-na-Gig over the southern doorway. This object is called in Irish *Sheila-na-Gioch*, which means Sheila-of-the-Breasts but

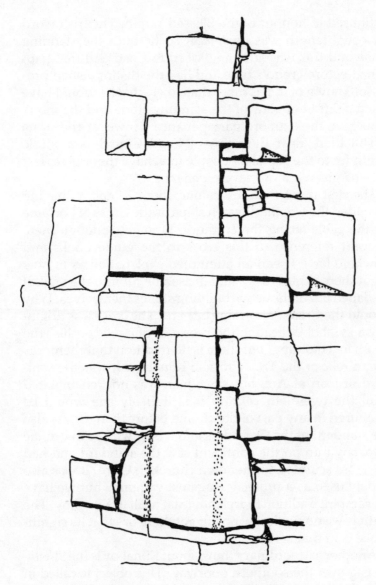

Cross of Lorraine in Kilnaboy

this does not make sense since there are no breasts exposed. It is a rather crude representation of a nude woman with her legs wide open exposing her genital organs to the public coming in to pray. Now what did all this mean? There has been an immense amount of scholarly waffle written about these sculptured pieces, most of it only helping to confuse the issue. Our Sheilas in Ireland are only part of a great European tradition of erotic art which reached its zenith in the middle ages. These figures were most probably introduced to Ireland by the Normans as a protection against evil. At that time European superstition attributed great protective powers to the female genitals which were seen, not as something revolting, but as the very source of life. A woman exposing her genitals was believed to be able to ward off the devil, prevent famine and floods, stop aggression and even cure sickness. This has been well illustrated by mediaeval woodcuts and later prints, the most notable being Eisen's illustration of La Fontaine in which an attractive young girl is shown raising her skirts to the horror of the Devil who makes a quick departure.

In Britain and on the continent these figures were called 'idols' but like so many other things the Irish adapted them to their own terminology. In ancient Ireland the epithet Sheila-na-Gig was applied to a loose woman or what was commonly called a Tally Woman, or in polite society 'slightly shop-soiled'; the word gig meaning in Irish 'frivolous' or 'flirtatious'. As time passed folk tradition gave this name to the 'idols'. While I simply cannot imagine a present-day bishop or parish priest putting the nude figure of Marilyn Munroe with her legs wide open over the entrance to his church, things may well have been different in ancient Ireland.

Probably our biggest difficulty in trying to understand the symbols of the past is our great ignorance of the outlook and mentality of the people of the time. We tend to judge them from the milieu in which we live. They had no news-papers, no radio, no TV, no telephones, no magazines, no postal service, no means of fast communication. The major-ity were unable to read or write. Like all human beings in such isolation they developed a high degree of superstition – or what appears to us as superstition but which was very real to them. It may well be that the Irish of a few hundred years hence will refer to the media and the TV as the super-stitions of our generation. The meaning of superstition is purely a matter of opinion.

When Christianity came to Ireland this superstition did not wane. The form of Christian instruction they got was laden with superstition. Instead of burning hay and bushes in stone circles we were now burning incense in churches. It is little wonder then that they took over the trappings of paganism and if the Sheila-na-Gig was a kind of protection against evil spirits, why should they not take it over even if it came centuries later. Surely the female genitals are as worthy a protection against evil as a plaster statue? Do we really have a clue as to what the ancient Irish were like or how their minds worked? Did they see in the sexual organs another example of the wonderful works of God, symbols of creation and of man's foretaste of eternal ecstasy? Is it possible that we are light years behind their perspective of life's purpose and meaning?

I do, however, have a little problem. I am told that not only are there female Sheila-na-Gigs but there are also male counterparts which have been given the name Mickey Magairle which means Testicle Mickey. I do not know how widespread the male version is but I have seen one. It is a sculptured stone with a massive male penis and testicles as big as hurling balls. It is hidden under a lot of bushes on the eastern side of Derrynaflan island where the wonder-ful chalice was found recently. What is its history? What is

Kilnaboy, Sheila-na-Gig in south wall

its meaning? Again we simply do not know.

In the puritanical purge which came after the Reformation many Sheila-na-Gigs were destroyed, principally by the clergy who probably saw in them a temptation to licentiousness. More of them were buried in out-of-the-way churchyards. Later on a lot more were wisely collected and brought to the National Museum in Dublin where they still remain. I was told a delightful story about the collection in the museum. It seems as if in the early days of the state they were being transferred from one room to another and to get there had to be brought through the offices where

41

there were a number of young civil servants, male and female. A kindly and discreet official, long since dead, felt it would be wrong to expose the young people to such unseemly sights and he ordered a collection of nappies to be put on the Sheilas. They were then duly transported through the offices without giving offence. What intrigues me most about this is what the Department of Finance said when they got a bill for a few dozen nappies from the National Museum.

Looking around Kilnaboy one can see that it was not just a church but was a great monastic convent site as well. One can see traces of the past in the surrounding fields. The cells of the nuns were made of wattles and probably thatched, which meant that they were warm in winter and cool in summer. These cells have long since vanished but sometimes a wattle took root and a tree or bush was born. Over the centuries this gave birth to more trees and bushes so that today, by careful observation one may see the rough lines of what the settlement was like.

Just north of the church the remains of a round tower can be seen. These round towers were primarily look-out posts and their presence usually indicated the existence of a fairly large settlement. Kilnaboy was no anchorite's retreat but it seems to have been a large and extensive convent of considerable importance.

I suppose there is in every one of us an incurable romantic streak. When I was growing up I used to fall in love with names; that is, I attributed to a woman all the magic which the musical sound of her name connotated. Deirdre of the Sorrows won my undying love as did Dervorgilla who ran away from her boorish husband all in the cause of true love. Had either of them been called Lizzie I would hardly have given them a second thought. My grand passion, however, was for Queen Maeve who exposed her breasts to distract the attention of Cuchulainn in battle and who offered that which could be found 'between her hips' to anyone who would slay him. My love for Maeve lasted the longest until one day I read in the *Táin* an account of her urinating. Apart from the fact that I had idealised her well above that sort of thing, I was shattered to learn that when she was finished her water made 'three great trenches in each of which a household could fit'. Somehow after that my love diminished.

All this leads me to a beautiful summer's day many years ago when here in the remains of this holy place I sat by the wall of the graveyard with my beloved dog, Maxie, lying by my side. It was a lovely July evening. A soft tender wind ruffled my hair and the air was filled with tranquillity and peace. All around me were the graves of the dead, and I remembered the words of the poet:

> Leaves have their time to fall
> And flowers to wither at the north wind's breath,
> And start to set – but all,
> Thou hast all seasons for thine own,
> Oh Death!

I closed my eyes, relaxed my body and drifted into a reverie. I slowly banished all thoughts and let impressions only have free reign. I was hoping that I would be able to roll back in time to the days when the chanting of psalms and the singing of hymns echoed through the dells of Kilnaboy. But it didn't work. It never does when one tries to force it. Instead there was one word, one impression jumping into my consciousness and it would not go away. It was the musical word 'Innerwee'. Was I going to love again? She slowly began to take shape in my mind, a thing of infinite beauty like a portrait that had been painted with loving care by an artist from heaven. Her presence became so powerful that I took fright. How crazy can one get, I thought. After all she was a nun, and probably an abbess. I jumped up and made for the car, smartly followed by Maxie. As I drove down the road I turned my head the other way as I passed by Innerwee's chair, a rock just inside the wall reported to cure troubles of the heart. I was afraid I might be tempted to sit on it and if I did the Lord knows what might have happened to me. I acted on the old proverb: 'He who fights and runs away, will live to fight another day,' and as I sped on my way as swiftly as I could towards Leamaneagh, I knew I was no longer young.

Dearest Innerwee! Even though you are a thousand years dead you are still alive. Forgive me if I ran away from the vision of your beauty. It was too much for an old man weary and tired of hopes which vanished like 'snow flakes on the desert's dusty face'. Other visions less attractive are beckoning me and I can see them faintly emerging over the soft distant horizon. Could it be that we might meet there in reality? But whisper, my dearest, is there any truth in the rumour that before you entered the convent you were the cause of frisky Teige O'Brien having to erect the standing stone in a field at Kilnaboy? I heard it talked about in a pub in Corofin! But then, you can't always believe what you hear in Corofin.

A short way down the Leamaneagh road there is a wayside monument to Albert O'Brien who was shot in 1923 by Free State soldiers. This little headstone evokes all the terrible tragedy of those far-off days. The Civil War was provoked and fuelled by the British in order to ensure that a government subservient to their interests would rule in Ireland. Poor Albert O'Brien was one of the thousands of Irishmen who had to pay the price of this piece of foreign policy with his life. The real tragedy is that he was an innocent man. It was a case of mistaken identity and the soldiers who shot him thought he was someone else.

There is something frightening about Leamaneagh Castle when it is approached from the south. It stands on a height, silhouetted against the sky and it has all the appearance of a castle from which one would expect Dracula to emerge at any moment. Inside its walls you get an eerie feeling as if it were an evil place. Even in Máire Rua's day it is said it was the kind of house where you never knew whether you were a guest or a victim.

Leamaneagh was the residence of Conor O'Brien and his wife Máire Rua. By all accounts Máire Rua was something which in modern parlance one would call a bitch. When her servants did something out of the way she punished them by hanging them by the hair of the head for a half-an-hour from the castle's gargoyles. Her husband Conor, was mortally wounded by the British at the battle of Inchicronan in 1651. When the stretcher bearers brought him to the castle Máire refused to let them in. 'We have no room here for dead men,' she said. However when she was told he was not dead she relented and nursed him until he died in the early hours of the next morning. He was no sooner buried than she betook herself with all haste to Limerick to marry a British officer, Colonel Cooper, so that having a Protestant husband she could preserve the castle and its lands for her son, who all the while was besporting himself in London and writing to his mother asking for money 'to exercise myself at the dancing school'.

After a while she tired of poor Cooper and one morning when she was helping him to shave the razor slipped and his throat was cut.

She then married another British officer and some years

later when the two of them were strolling on the roof of the castle the unfortunate husband fell to the ground and was killed. Nothing daunted she married yet another British officer, and one fine summer's day Máire and himself were out riding at the Cliffs of Moher. The husband was riding Máire's charger and when they were at the edge of the cliffs Máire let out a strange whistle and her charger raised his hind quarters and threw the unfortunate husband over the cliff and into the sea. It has been remarked upon that she was not too successful in finding a fifth husband.

But as they say in Irish *Fíllean an feall ar an feallaire* (the evil deed returns on the doer). She evicted a poor widow from a little cottage for some flimsy reason and the widow went to the cursing stones near Carron, turned them towards Leamaneagh and cursed Máire Rua 'that she may die roaring with her legs in the air'. Sometime after that Máire was out hunting. Her horse took fright and bolted throwing her into a tree, her legs up and head down. That was how they found her – dead.

Máire Rua, however, was a prudent woman. She did not forget to keep an eye on the next world – just in case there was one. In her will she hoped to fix God by leaving large sums of money to the Abbey of Quin and the Dominican Convent in Limerick. She left a substantial stipend to each priest who 'celebrates Mass over my corpse'.

All the same she had her good points. She left Peter Arthur a grey horse, Sarah Quealy a cow and a heifer, a black pot and a griddle, Slaney Neylon a brass yellow pan and a big skillet. She remained a Catholic to the end, although she had her children brought up as Protestants. What a great book she could have written under the title: *How to Make the Best of Both Worlds*.

Leamaneagh Castle is not a place one lingers in. Even Maxie prefers to remain sitting outside the gate so perhaps it is better to move down the road a few miles to Kilfenora. Near Kilfenora there is a little stream called 'Banshees Brook' and sometimes in very wet weather the water gets red from an iron seam in the soil. This is a sign that the Banshee is around as she likes red water that looks like blood. The tradition of the Banshee is very strong in the Burren and most old people have heard her wailing. Some say that she is one of the fallen angels, others say she is the guardian angel of someone in hell. They say that when dogs start digging holes in the ground it's a sign she's coming. It is also said that deaf people can hear her. Nevertheless she's a decent sort of a person, by all accounts, who'd give you a drag on her chalk pipe or a pinch of snuff if you asked her nicely.

The first thing that strikes one about this charming village of Kilfernora is its cleanliness – clean gardens, clean houses, clean shops, clean streets. It is a homely, friendly cleanliness with none of the austerity one sees in continental villages of its size. It seems so perfectly natural and traditional. It is a cleanliness that is in absolute good taste. One can also see that a tremendous effort has been made to bring Kilfenora into the twentieth century without losing one iota of its historic past. To quote from George Cunningham's excellent *Burren Journey*:

Kilfenora (pop. 125) is now a thriving market village with a reasonable tourist trade and a focal point for Burren development. Not too long ago this area presented a depressing picture with untarred roads, no amenities, and a lack of essential services. A concentrated local effort encouraged the local authority to improve the situation with properly surfaced link roads and basic services such as a new water supply. These improvements prompted the formation of a Co-operative movement to promote and develop the potential of the Burren: Comhar Connradh na Boirne. . .

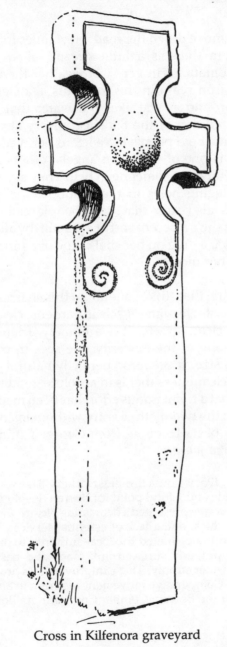

Cross in Kilfenora graveyard

It is the old, old story. Do it yourself – the government won't do it for you – especially if it is of an Irish historical nature. Here one can see our slave mind in action. Our governments have starved centres like Kilfenora of funds while literally millions of pounds are available to restore British institutions like the Royal Hospital, Kilmainham or the Clanrickard Castle in Portumna.

Comhar Connradh na Boirne has revitalised Kilfenora – especially in opening the Burren Display Centre where they have recreated the flora, fauna and structure of the Burren in wax and silk models. A visit to this centre introduces one to the magnificence of the area and to what is worth seeing and where to find it.

Anytime I have visited Kilfenora in recent years so crowded was the little square that I had difficulty in parking. Cars from France, Germany, Holland, large touring buses, including one from far-away Vienna, filled almost all the spaces. Where a village, or indeed a nation, is proud of its historical past the world bows in admiration.

Where the Cathedral now stands there was once a monastery but it seems to have been plundered and burned early in the twelfth century. Shortly afterwards the Cathedral was built on the same site and its earliest records go back to 1189. It was of course a diocese in its own right, the diocese of Kilfenora and Kilmacduagh, until it was amalgamated with Galway because there was not enough money to pay two episcopal administrations – at least that was the excuse. It had a long line of distinguished bishops but for me the eccentric Patrick Fallon is the most interesting and colourful.

When Fallon entered Maynooth as a clerical student he was not sure if he had ever been baptised a Catholic, so they had to do the job there and then in case his suspicions were correct. He was eventually ordained and became parish priest of Lisdoonvarna where he was especially noted for his care of the poor. During the famine he wrote passionate and appealing letters to the Chief Secretary in Dublin to help the starving people of Lisdoonvarna. There were 5,000 of them and only 30 had jobs. But to no avail. The British administration in Dublin let them die.

Old Bishop French died in 1852 and in those days the parish priests elected the new bishop. The procedure was that three names were sent to Rome and the Pope chose. The order of merit was designated Dignissimus, Dignissima and Dignissimum. Fallon was elected the Dignissimus and after a lot of ecclesiastical wrangling he was appointed Bishop.

For a number of years he did a great job in revitalising the diocese, building churches and schools and then he got the notion that he was not a properly consecrated bishop and he had the job done again, this time on the quiet. As the years passed he got a little too fond of the bottle and constant complaints were being sent to Rome that he was too often drunk in public, particularly in the company of Liscannor fishermen, that he was too besotted to attend to the welfare of the diocese, and worst of all that his bosom companion was one Corney O'Brien who was living with a woman not his wife – 'in concubinage' as they called it at the time. Eventually poor Fallon was persuaded to retire and he spent his last years in a monastery in Dublin where the liquor was scarce and the prayers were plentiful.

Rome used the Fallon saga to amalgamate the diocese of Kilfenora with that of Galway where a somewhat stricter regime was in operation.

The Cathedral itself is well covered by the guide books but you will heighten your appreciation and understanding if you try to visualise what it was like in its days of glory. The chancel was roofed and it had a wooden ceiling painted blue with golden stars. Since the Irish were great lovers of colour almost everything inside would have been painted in one shade or another. So close your eyes and picture what it was like. I venture to suggest that no modern psychedelic disco had such wonderful variety of hues and tones. In Kilfenora they were ascending as silent prayers and not as confusing symbols. Then it was a secret place of peace and love and understanding.

Outside we run into another great mystery – the high crosses. An immense amount of waffle has been written about the purpose of these high crosses. The truth is that nobody really knows their precise function. One theory holds that they were merely decorative monuments to the ego-mania of worldly clerics. Another theory is that because of the illiteracy of the people they were used to instruct them in the gospels at sermon time on Sundays.

It may well be that some were instructional and some decorative but in general there are a number of interesting aspects to these crosses that may not strike one at first glance.

High crosses became popular in many parts of Europe as a form of devotion to the True Cross which was supposed to have been found earlier near Jerusalem. Later this was celebrated by the introduction into the liturgy of the Feast of the Exaltation of the Holy Cross. This distinct oriental flavour can be seen on many of the Irish high crosses. The caps, for instance, have Armenian features. Did the eastern stone-cutters come to Ireland or did our stone-cutters go there? It seems that we had contact very early on with the orient. There is an account in the *Tain* of Cuchulainn 'travelling as far as the mountains of Armenia' and much later we read that one of the founders of Rahan and Killeigh monasteries was Cerrui from Armenia. How this oriental influence came about is really unknown. Another

Large cross in Kilfenora churchyard, east face

unanswered question is why the high crosses passed the main countries of Europe by. They seem to have taken root only in Ireland, Scotland and parts of England, as well as in Armenia and Georgia.

If we relate the early Irish litanies and prayers to the scenes on the crosses we find that in many cases the scenes invoked in the prayers are those depicted on the crosses. This could suggest that the prayers were recited in public in front of the crosses or that, as well, individual monks or nuns strolling around the gardens might contemplate the scenes as they prayed. Again there is no certainty.

It is estimated that thousands of such crosses were scattered throughout the country. Many were destroyed by the invading British at the time of the Reformation, others were hidden and then lost. Still others simply fell down and and became embedded in the earth. What seems very probable however is that each monastic settlement had more than a few. Some probably for teaching the people, some for inspirational purposes and some, like Clonmacnoise, erected to the memory of some famous Abbot. Even then human nature was weak enough to think that large commemorative memorials counted for something in the next world.

I think it is reasonably certain that Kilfenora had several crosses scattered around the grounds of the settlement. Only three now remain, and the various motifs of these are so complicated as to defy rational explanation. These high crosses in their hey-day were all painted in a variety of colours, like the inside of the Cathedral. Kilfenora must have been a wonderful sight in those days. The settlement took in the village and surrounding fields. There were the coloured crosses, perhaps scores of them, the Cathedral, the monk's cells made of wattle, the well laid-out grounds with gardens and flowers, shrubs and trees. Isolated as it then was it must have been one of the secret places of the Burren. The Kilfenora monastic site is a tourist amenity today and not really a place of quiet peaceful prayer. This surely suggests that it might be usefully restored. Such places as have been restored like Holy Cross and Ballin-tubber are visited each year by hundreds of thousands of visitors and apart from being aesthetically pleasing are very successful commercial ventures. But this takes vision and vision is a scarce commodity amongst our legislators. Most probably, if it is ever done, it will be by the people of Kilfenora themselves. It is by no means an impossible dream and by no means beyond the capabilities of these imaginative and progressive people.

Kilfenora church, detail of east window

THREE

ROCKS ARE HIS
WRITTEN WORDS

I see His face in every flower.
The thunder and the singing of the birds
Are but His voice – and carven by His
*   power*
Rocks are His written words.
                        JOSEPH PLUNKETT

Lisdoonvarna is not one of the most secret places of the Burren. Indeed it is one of the most public but it has a very secret activity – matchmaking.

It is quite a modern town which grew up in the last century around the spa wells which are reputed to have health-giving properties, especially in the cure of rheumatism – an ailment which in the past afflicted farmers and parish priests and others prone to wettings. Indeed in the 1920s Lisdoonvarna was described as the town where the 'parish priests tried to look sober and the farmers tried to look drunk'. Now that all the priests have cars and no longer get wettings on sick calls, they have deserted it for the golf course of Lahinch. But the farmers have remained loyal and true. From the end of August to the beginning of October they come in their thousands to 'take the waters' and, where applicable, to search for a wife.

Because of the latter activity which is pursued with great secrecy, Lisdoonvarna has acquired the name of a match-making town. Professional, semi-professional and amateur matchmakers are readily and discreetly available to lend a guiding hand to the course of true love by bringing together bashful maidens and hopeful bachelors from the farmlands of Ireland.

I did not realise how secretive all this was until I decided to try it out for myself, not indeed for a wife but for the crack. I dressed up in a navy-blue suit, white shirt, brown tie, brilliantine in my hair and I let it be known around the town that I was a strong farmer with a hundred acres of good land and that I was willing. Days passed and nothing happened. I sat alone in pubs casting furtive glances at giggling groups of rosy-cheeked farmers's daughters but they looked past me as if I did not exist. As a last resort I tried to make a direct approach to some matchmakers but none could be found to take on my case. It was only then I found out what was wrong. Word had perculated through the grapevine that I was not a farmer, but a writer looking for copy and that I had already written not very complimen-tary things about matchmaking in a book. My informant kindly confided in me that if I wished to remain in good health it might be advisable to move on. I took his advice. I still have the navy-blue suit – any offers?

The incident referred to was in my book *The Wind that Round the Fastnet Sweeps* where I recounted meeting a pro-fessional matchmaker who tried to fix me up with a well-to-do widow. His main selling point was that she had a bad stammer and, he said, this was a great advantage since she could not answer me back when we would be having a row. This man, one of the last of his breed, told me of the nature of his work which possibly is as applicable in the Burren as in West Cork:

'Suppose there was an ould couple with two sons,' he said. 'Well the eldest would get the farm and as soon as the ould couple got the pension they'd give a fistful of money to the next fellow so that he could get a woman and marry into her farm. He'd come to me then and I'd have to find a woman with a dacent bit of land. More than likely she'd have her father and mother livin' with her. I'd ramble up to them on a Sunday evening by way of no harm. We'd talk about the weather and politics and the price of pigs and anything else that would come into our minds. Mind you they'd know bloody well what I was there for. The girl would be all shy and red in the face and after a while she'd gather herself up into the room out of the way and then I'd tell the ould couple I had word of a match. Himself would want to know who the fellow was and how much he had. I'd mention a figure well below what we had in mind so as to give myself a bit of room for bargaining. If he was agreeable he'd say he'd want a lot more but we could talk about that later. Then the next Sunday, when the mother and daughter would be gone to second mass, I'd call up with me bould bachelor and himself and meself and the girl's father would walk the land. We'd have to do that to satisfy my man that he wasn't getting a pig in a poke, and that the land was well fenced, and watered, with no ragworth, thistles or boucha-launs. We'd have a look at the outhouses and all the stock and if my man was satisfied then I'd arrange with the girl's father to come another day by myself to talk about the arrangements. Man alive 'tis then the trouble would start and I might have to make several journeys before we'd finally fix on the sum of money the bachelor would bring with him. Anyway when we had all that fixed we'd name a day to go to town to draw up the writings. You see we'd have to go to a solicitor to put everything in writin'. You could never trust the word of a mountainy farmer, for he's so crooked that if he said the rosary with you he'd try to do you out of a decade. Anyway we'd all go to town, meself, the bachelor, the girl with her father and mother into a solicitor's office and everything would be put down on paper. The farm would be made over to the two when they married, the dowry would be lodged in the bank in the two names, the ould couple would have the right to be fed and to keep their pension, and they'd also have a right to one room in the house and a seat in the car to mass on Sunday, and a whole lot of other things like that. Then they'd all have to write their names on the piece of paper the solicitor would put in front of them and when that was over we'd go to an eatin' house for a feed of pig's head and cabbage and after that into the best pub in town for a bit of a celebration. We'd try to leave the couple alone so as they'd get to know one another. At first they'd be very shy and he'd be lookin' at her like a cat studying a saucer of boiled milk. After a while they'd soften out and he'd start to call her by her first name and from there on they'd be no stoppin' the two of them'.

He also told me that his payment would be two shillings in the pound of the dowry money and two shillings in the pound of the value of the stock. That, of course, was the old style, where the young couple had no choice. This Lisdoonvarna system, I am told, is somewhat more sophisticated, and the young people have complete say in the choice of partner. But otherwise the procedure runs on similar lines.

The old matchmaker told me that out of approximately four hundred matches he made during the course of his life there were only two failures. One was where the man went a bit 'quare in the head' and had to be committed to an asylum. The other is best told in the matchmaker's own words:

Any man over fifty that would come to me looking for a wife I'd ask him to strip off first, to make sure his machinery was in order, before I'd make a move. You see I made a match between a cobbler and a respectable farmer's daughter a few years ago, who had £2,000 and brought it with her. A month after the wedding she came to me in a flaring temper and demanded back the money she paid me for making the match, for she said he spent the whole month on top of her grunting and farting but couldn't do a damn thing. One night when he was in a drunken sleep she pulled back the bedclothes, took down the Sacred Heart lamp and had a good look at him. Well, according to her what he had was so small that she had to put on her spectacles to see it. She left him there and then and I had to give her back the fee she paid me for she claimed I sold her defective goods. Ever since then I insist on inspecting things for myself to make sure the necessary implements are there and in good order too.

Now all this may sound archaic and at times humorous, but it has a very serious side insofar as it brings into sharp focus the whole concept of modern marriage in Ireland. According to those who ought to know, such as clergy, counsellors, doctors, social workers, some seventy-five percent of Irish married couples barely tolerate each other and stay together in this hateful relationship mainly because of the children. These figures, it was pointed out to me however, applied largely to cities and towns. In rural Ireland the percentages might well be reversed.

I once asked an intelligent priest who ministered in a city parish if he ever regretted not having chosen a different career and having married. His answer was quite revealing: 'Every human being would like to love and be loved by a woman, and through that love to create a family of one's own flesh. But having experienced so many wrecked and broken marriages in my pastoral duties, I can truly say that from a human point of view I am glad I never married. I have no reason to believe I would have fared better than the rest. Today when I attend a wedding breakfast, which should be an occasion of happiness and joy, I am overwhelmed by sadness. As I look into the glowing faces of the young couple, full of love and happiness, I know that all the chances are that in a few years I will be called in to try and patch up their marriage, destroyed by hatred and greed. It has happened to me over and over again. No! I think I really chose the easier part.'

What all this adds up to is that the chances of failure in the romantic love match are dangerously high while the chances of failure in the arranged match are comparatively low. Why should this be so? This book is not, thank God, a treatise on marriage but one cannot write about Lisdoonvarna and leave it out so perhaps a few comments may be offered. Some say that the reason is that in romantic love we expect everything and get nothing, while in the arranged match we expect nothing and get everything. Others say that romantic love is a cruel trick of nature to promulgate the human race, has nothing to do with marriage and should be tried out many times to get it out of one's system. My own view is that it goes somewhat deeper. Marriage is a vital part of life. If one's life is based on inordinate egoism, self love and greed, then any marriage will fail, no matter how it came about. I have noticed over the years a far greater degree of greed and selfishness in the cities and towns than in the rural areas where a friendly neighbourly spirit prevails. Why this should be so I do not know unless it is because the more we get the greedier we get. But it is a harsh reality that one has got to accept. Unlike the past when a lot of idealism prevailed, most of our betters today are motivated by greed and this perculates down along more quickly and strongly in the cities and more slowly in the rural areas. If my theory is right then there is little hope for marriage until the problem of greed is tackled first. How that can be done is one of the most urgent problems facing our church leaders and educationalists. End of Lecture!

Benjamin Disraeli had an extremely happy marriage. When he was very old he brought his wife Mary Anne out for dinner one evening and during the course of the meal he said to her:

'You know Mary Anne, when I married you I married you for your money and for your influence and power which made me prime minister of England.'

'I know that,' answered Mary Anne quietly.

'But I want to say this,' continued Disraeli. 'If I were to marry you again I would marry you for love.'

'I know that too,' replied the happy Mary Anne.

So before plunging too deeply into a romantic alliance perhaps a little holiday in Lisdoonvarna should be tried first. I wish you better luck than I had.

Lisdoonvarna is not just a town where matches are made but it is also a centre for much more sophisticated business and cultural affairs. Its new conference hall is one of the most up-to-date in the country and the numbers of good hotels and lively pubs ensure that delegates can unwind from their weighty problems when the day's work is done.

For a number of years past the Cumann Merriman assemble here for their annual summer school. This conference is one which has attracted a lot of biting comments to the effect that it is the annual booze up of the Dublin 4 gaels, at the expense of Bord na Gaeilge, which of course is the Irish taxpayer. This I think is unfair. While there are a few regular attenders whose knowledge of the science of the gullet is superb, in general Cumann Merriman has shown itself to be a worth-while venture. It has helped in the publication of a few good books and occasionally it throws up an important issue, such as Patrick MacEntee's superb lecture recently on extradition. But one gets the impression that it is far too timid and it should be utilising the wonderful talent it has at its disposal in dealing with such themes as the Destruction of the Irish Language by Native Governments, the Brutality of the Northern Security Forces, the Subservience of our Government to Foreign Powers, etc.

These are burning issues and it is a great pity that such a fine organisation as Cumann Merriman does not bring them into public focus.

Merriman himself was of course a Clareman, born a few miles from Lisdoonvarna in 1750, and was the author of the wild, magnificent, erotic poem in the Irish language, *The Midnight Court*. It is rightly regarded as by far the most important contribution to Irish literature in the eighteenth century because of the richness of its language, the astonishing vocabulary of words with all their shades of meaning and the courage shown in handling the subject. Its theme is the Irishwoman's right to sex and marriage and the Irishman's inclination to consider the former but to avoid the latter at all costs. While one could say it is erotic rather than pornographic, it leaves little to the imagination as this short extract shows:

> But she would stretch out luxuriantly,
> Bit by bit his thoughts seducing,
> Side to side and her limbs around him,
> Mouth on mouth, pawing him downwards.
> Often around him she twined her foot;
> From his belt to his knee her brush she rubbed;
> She snatched from his loins the quilt and the blanket,
> With a cheerless old heap to play and dally.
> It's often she grasped his lifeless sceptre
> And rubbed its mouth to her groin in frenzy,
> Took it within her soft hand nimbly,
> And roused not the wretch to excitement or business.

This little extract comes from a delightful paperback *The Midnight Court* edited and translated by Dr Patrick C. Power. This is a dual-language book with Irish on the left-hand pages and English on the opposite pages. It is a particularly interesting edition because it contains seventy-five lines which are absent from most other editions. It was quite understandable that these lines should be omitted in the past since by naming certain people and their mis-demeanours they could be held to be gravely libellous. Dr Power not only brings his great scholarship to bear on this translation but presents it in a most readable and acceptable form and for those who understand Irish it is intriguing to compare both versions.

Lisdoonvarna very nearly became the Dallas of Ireland in 1878. In January of that year *The Munster News* reported the discovery of oil there. A Patrick MacInerney, a baker who was building a new house on the mail car road to Ennis struck a rock from which there gushed a copious flow of oil resembling paraffin and when a match was put to it it ignited and 'gave forth a brilliant light'. Nothing more seems to have been heard of the find which is probably no harm. After all who would want to destroy Lisdoonvarna with all its wonderful hostelries, pubs, delightful secluded walks and charming people, as the Kinvara poet Francis A. Fahy recorded:

> All sorts and conditions
> Of men on all missions
> Are there to be found.
> There are jobbers and teachers
> And pedlars and preachers
> And delicate creatures from all Ireland round
> There are blooming young maidens
> And hearts heavy laden
> And stout dames that no sign of fading yet showed.
> While dearly doomed daughters
> Are trying the waters
> Along the bog road.

The little road from Lisdoonvarna to Doolin winds in and out and up and down as if in sympathy with the rugged landscape. There is a happiness about it especially in the early morning as if it were glad to have come safely through the night to see the sun once more.

Doolin and the surrounding land and sea are steeped in history and culture. I always stop for a moment at the Church of the Holy Rosary to visit the graves of two friends of my youth who are buried in the nearby graveyard. This simple country church was built in 1830 on the site of a very famous Brehon Law School founded by the MacClancy family in about 1350. This school flourished and enjoyed a nation-wide reputation until one of the family, Boetius MacClancy, turned his coat and threw his lot in with the occupying British forces about 1580. He was rewarded by being appointed Sheriff of County Clare. One of his first acts was to abolish the Brehon Laws and institute British laws instead. In this way he put an end to the great Irish law school and to his family's heritage of two hundred years.

Like so many other Irishmen before and since, the said Boetius proved a dutiful quisling, not stopping at brutality and murder to ingratiate himself with his new masters. In 1588 a ship of the Armada was wrecked near Doolin pier. Most of the crew were drowned but about fifty managed to fight the high seas and scramble ashore. Famished and half starving, Boetius arrested them one by one as they struggled among the rocks. He assembled them all and hung them on a small hillock a short distance east of the Church of the Holy Rosary known to this day as Cnocan an Chrocaire, the Hanging Hillock. MacClancy is said to have hidden a vast hoard of gold somewhere near here. The only clue given is: *Trí léim lachan ó lic na habhánn* (Three jumps of a duck from the stone of the river). If you can decipher this cryptic clue a fortune may be yours.

Further down the road at a little suburb of Doolin called

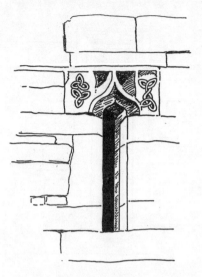

Window in Toomullin Church

Fisher Street there is a magnificent bridge over the Aille
River. On the south-east beside MacDermot's pub, a car
track leads to an unusual fifteenth century church ruin
known as Toomullin Church. Little is known about this
church. It looks as if it had been a small settlement of three
or four monks. Nearby are the remains of the usual holy
well, St Brecan's, with the remnants of rags, medals, coins
etc. left there by more modern pilgrims.

Many years ago I was with a class from the Burren Paint-
ing Centre exercising our artistic skills in the vicinity of this
ancient church. During the lunch break another student
and myself made our way through the nettles and rubble
into the little ruins. It was an eerie place with the smell of
death. About six or seven feet up one of the walls I noticed
a large, loose, protruding stone and, in the hope of finding
a Derrynaflan Chalice and making my fortune, I removed
the stone. There was, unfortunately, no chalice but what I

Window in Toomullin Church

found there was something hardly ever discovered before in the ruins of a fifteenth century Irish church. It was a copy of the current issue of *Playboy* magazine with full compliment of nudes in colour. How did it get there? After some ribald discussion we came to the conclusion that it was put there either by some young lad hiding it from his mother or some old farmer using it to arouse his flagging prowess when he had an assignment in the isolated ruin. It was early in May and we were in the frivolous mood of spring with devilment not very far away. We slipped quietly back to the car, drove to the church where we bought a pamphlet entitled *The Virtue of Holy Purity*. In red and blue crayon we underlined all the relative phrases about chaste thoughts, custody of the eyes, immodest jokes etc. and then put the pamphlet behind the stone in the ruin. We debated whether or not we should keep the magazine but decided to return it to the cavity having first written the words 'Prepare to meet thy doom' in large red letters across the cover. I would dearly love to know the end of the story. How did the owner feel when he came upon this unusual find? Perhaps we may have been responsible for a major miracle. Perhaps the young lad, if it were a young lad, gave up his promiscuous desires and joined a religious order. Perhaps the old farmer got married, having decided that a bed was a safer and more congenial place, as well as having the grace of God with him in holy matrimony. Who knows? Over a pint in MacDermot's pub we comforted ourselves with the old proverb: 'God writes straight with crooked lines' – we being the crooked lines.

The whole Doolin area must have been a major centre of population two thousand years ago. It is teeming with early monuments, graves, places of worship, ring forts and standing stones. The past rises up in every field. The history and archaeology of Doolin merits an entire book unto itself. Many of the Christians buidings were erected on the ruins of old pagan monuments. Pope Gregory the Great issued a directive on this:

The idol temples should not be destroyed. If the shrines are well built it is important that they should be changed from the worship of the devil to the service of the true God.

One church, however, the fifteenth century Killilagh Church with its beautiful windows and strange ogee-headed openings is well worth a visit. It brings one back in vivid terms to those tragic days of the sixteenth and seventeenth centuries when such churches were burned to the ground, their coffers plundered and their monks put to death.

Nearby is the large MacNamara tomb where it is said

that no one is buried but which was used as a prison by the IRA during the War of Independence. Here in this graveyard local tradition has it that the great Patrick Sarsfield attended the funeral of his ADC but I have not yet been able to find his grave.

Doolin House is no longer there. It was a MacNamara residence and during the War of Independence Henry Valentine MacNamara lived there. He sided with the British while his son who lived nearby sided with the Irish. When the IRA shot Henry Valentine the British burned Doolin House as a reprisal!

With certain reservations which I shall mention later Doolin can be regarded as one of the secret places of the Burren. If you leave the village and pier behind you and stroll along the rocks towards the north you will find wonderful inlets of peace and tranquillity hidden between glistering sheltering rocks. I remember one day I found a secret place not far from the pier.

It was a beautiful scene. The midday sun was shedding its rays on the clear blue sea. The Aran islands came up out of the distance like mediaeval serpents. Away on the horizon the twelve pins of Connemara stood out against a radiant sky. My only companions were Maxie, who lay beside me, and the beautiful sea gulls poised overhead. As I admired these graceful creatures of God I remembered Gerald Griffin's ethereal poem written a century and a half ago on the seagulls he saw almost in the same spot where I was sitting:

> White bird of the tempest! O beautiful thing!
> With the bosom of snow and the motionless wing
> Now sweeping the billow, now floating on high
> Now bathing thy plumes in the light of the sky
> Now silently poised o'er the war of the main,
> Like the spirit of Charity brooding o'er pain

Thou seem'st to my spirit, as upwards I gaze,
And see thee, now clothed in mellowest rays,
Now lost in the storm-driven vapours that fly
Like hosts that are rooted across the broad sky.

As I sat there quietly enjoying my lunch and sharing it with Maxie, my thoughts turned to the great cultural tradition which permeates Doolin and its people. J. M. Synge was a regular visitor. So too was Augustus John, George Bernard Shaw, Dylan Thomas and many others.

Of all these Synge was perhaps the greatest. Born of an ascendancy family he soon tired of the arid emptiness of his class, their shallowness and their toadyism and he became an Irish nationalist in the fullest sense of the word. Shortly after his death, and when he had become famous, it became fashionable to say that he was not a real nationalist as it is now fashionable to say that Michael Collins, Dan Breen and Liam Lynch were constitutional politicians, but his friend Stephen McKenna wrote of him:

As regards political interests, I would die for the theory that Synge was almost intensely nationalist. He habitually spoke with rage and bitter hateful eyes of the English in Ireland. . . . he wanted as dearly as he wanted anything to see Ireland quite free.

Again Synge himself describes the deep state of pain and anger at seeing the RIC descend on the Aran Islands, just as young Irishmen in the Six Counties might feel at the sight of a lorry load of RUC disgorging in Belfast:

When the anchor had been thrown it gave me a strange throb of pain to see the boats being lowered and the sunshine gleaming on the rifles and helmets of the constabulary who crowded into them.

The turning point in Synge's life came after a long talk

ts at the Hotel Corneille in Paris. Yeats said
ip Paris; you will never create anything by
. . . Go to the Aran Islands. Live there as if
of the people themselves; express a life that
has never found expression.' That is exactly what Synge
did.

He went to the Aran Islands. He shared life in a cottage
with the people. He learned their language and became a
fluent speaker. He experienced with them their privations
and sorrows as well as their meagre infrequent joys. Slowly
he discovered the depth of their being.

This sojourn in the Aran Islands purged his mind of any
idea that the English or the Anglo-Irish were superior.
Living amongst these poverty-stricken, suppressed people
he unearthed a dignity, an otherworldliness, a culture
going back thousands of years. He also learned, as Yeats
told him, that they were not expressed in literature in the
same way as the English peasant was given expression by
Hardy, the French peasant by Balzac, the Russian peasant
by Turgenev. On the contrary where literary expression
was given to them it was an ignorant caricature designed
to amuse British and Anglo-Irish drawing rooms – the 'be-
gorra, be jaysus, top-of-the-morning, yer honour' so
beloved by Somerville and Ross, Maria Edgeworth, Charles
Lever, Samuel Lover and a host of other writers who
exploited the Irish for fame and amusement. Far from
exploiting them Synge explored out of love and respect and
discovered the untold cultural riches that lay hidden
beneath the surface. It was this deep understanding and
sensibility which gave the world one of the greatest plays
in the English language – *Riders to the Sea*.

If Synge were to set *Riders to the Sea* in Doolin he would
hardly need to change a line. They were the same people.
They lived only a few miles apart. They suffered the same

privations trying to wrest a living from a savage sea that claimed the lives of so many of their young men and left so many of their women widows and their children orphans. They spoke the same language – Doolin was Irish speaking when Synge was alive. The same folktales and legends were recounted again and again at their firesides. They were part of the same age-old culture.

It was not, however, the oral tradition that made Synge such a frequent visitor to Doolin. It was the music of Doolin that attracted him. The entire west Clare area is a rich repository of folk music. In this it differs from the rest of Ireland. Why that should be is a question for the anthropologist. Doolin is, and has ever been, one of the rich pockets of this traditional music. Few know that Synge studied music at Trinity and had become an expert on the flute, violin and piano. One can understand why the music of Doolin, so wild and lively, so expressive of the landscape, should attract him. At one stage of his life he toyed with the idea of becoming a composer but ultimately opted for literature. Who knows, had he become a composer, what he might have done with the strange haunting folk music of west Clare.

Doolin still preserves the great tradition of folk music but unfortunately in recent years it is invaded each summer by swarms of beardies and their weirdies, not because of any real love of music, but because it is the 'in thing' to do. You can see them every day during July and August suffocating the place with their filthy jeans and Lech Wallesa moustaches, wallowing in dirt because this way they think they can draw attention to themselves.

Earlier I said I had certain reservations about Doolin. Doolin can still be experienced as a secret place if one avoids going there in July and August while these hoards are around. Doolin still has the music, the musicians and the wonderful people, but try to go there in May or June or late September or October. You will then be able to experience Doolin as Synge experienced it and that experience is really worth while. But a word of warning. Doolin may well grip you and hold you longer than you intended. Many times in the past I have gone there intending to stay a few hours and then surfaced days later wondering where I had been. *Caveat Emptor*.

Before you leave Doolin slip over to the Cliffs of Moher – they are only a few miles away. Not only will you enjoy the view, but you will find there a delightful restaurant-cum-craft shop, with a lovely impressive selection of books about Ireland. You can browse or buy as you will.

Ballinlacken Castle, a few miles north-east of Doolin, is set in a position of scenic beauty surrounded by green foliage so absent in many other parts of the Burren. But it is also set in a strategic defensive position and the view from the top of the castle covers all possible approaches. The castle itself dates from the sixteenth century and is much the same as the ordinary run of these castles. It does seem however that this castle was built on the site of a very much older defensive position – perhaps dating back to the earliest settlers in Ireland.

Like all others it has its quota of grim stories. One of these concerned Mahon O'Brien who was murdered in 1565 by his cousins who lived on the Aran Islands. Mahon's son, Donal, with a few retainers, made a foray into the islands and captured the assassins. They brought them in chains to Ballinlacken and from a point where they could see Aran, they hanged some and burned others. Such O'Briens were obviously men not to be trifled with.

Ballinlacken House situated close to the castle, now a well known guest house, was once the home of the notorious Lord Peter O'Brien (1842-1914). O'Brien's career is of special interest, not because of his distinction as a lawyer, but because he is an excellent example of a specific type of Irishman who placed his talents at the disposal of the British in his own occupied country. Without people like O'Brien the British could never have ruled Ireland for so long. On the continent of Europe these people were regarded as traitors and were shot. In recent times they were given the name 'Quisling' after a Norwegian who became the tool of the invader. In Ireland, however, by a skilful combination of propaganda, patronage and exploitation of the slave mind, society was persuaded to accept these betrayers and indeed very often to honour them. No other country in the world displayed such servility as we then displayed and indeed display today. We have become so used to slavery that we have come to love our chains. Peter O'Brien is a perfect example of one of those quislings.

O'Brien died in 1914, laden with honours of every kind. Even the most distinguished Irishmen, such as Sir Horace Plunket, sang his praises. The nationalist Bishop of Killaloe, Dr Fogarty, wrote that the Irish people 'had a true and courageous friend who never forgot the country where he was born'. This is a sample of the level of acceptance which is incomprehensible to the mind of any self-respecting European. O'Brien's name is associated with malpractice and corruption so that he is best known as 'Peter the Packer'. He got this nickname from his ability to 'pack' juries, with people who thought like himself and so give the desired verdict to please his masters. Many innocent people were hanged, and others deported because of his dishonesty.

But the British pay their servants well, without enquiring too closely into their methods, and O'Brien went from Crown Prosecutor, to Attorney General, to the highest office of Lord Chief Justice. He had everything this world could give on his death bed. Yet he had to face a final judge himself – a judge who could not be bought or 'packed'. What the verdict of that court was can only be surmised. But his memory remains as a blot of shame on the Burren.

More enchanting even than the secret places are the secret roads that slip silently off the main tourist highways – the little roads of Eva Gore-Booth 'that go rambling through my heart'.

Shortly after leaving the main entrance to Ballinlacken Castle there is a turning to the right and this will bring you to one of the most secret roads – the Green Road – a road where a thousand years of history meets you on every turn. A short distance along this road a turn to the left will bring you to Oughtdarra where you can visit the ruins of St Mac-Dara's Church. Close by you will find one of the saddest of sights – a Killeen, or a graveyard for unbaptised children. There are many such graveyards in the Burren and each time I visit one I have difficulty in surpressing my anger. Up to the turn of the century babies who died before they were baptised were not permitted to be buried in consecrated ground. Which savage, inhuman eunuch in the Vatican thought up that demoniacal rule is unknown. The banishment of these innocent little children of God is surely a crime which hits rock bottom for insensitivity and lack of charity. Imagine the suffering parents, already grief-stricken by the reality of death, to have this added brutality inflicted on them in their hour of deepest sorrow. Instead, however, of dwelling on this monstrous act we can remember the gentle words of Christ: *Let the little children come to Me for theirs is the Kingdom of Heaven*. May they rest in peace in their little nameless graves. Here the words of John Clare written more than a hundred years ago come to mind:

Infants' gravemounds are steps of angels, where
Earth's brightest gems of innocence repose.
God is their parent so they need no tear.
He takes them to his bosom from earth's woes
A bud their lifetime and a flower their close.
Infants have nought to weep for ere they die.
All prayers are needless beads they need not tell;
White flowers their mourners are, Nature their passing Bell.

Come back again to the Green Road and travel north-wards as far as Ballynahown. The entire area westward to the sea is extremely rich in curious ancient monuments of various kinds. Indeed a whole day could be spent traversing this piece of landscape. There is Cathair na Greine, the Caher of the Sun, Caherdoon, the Caher of the Fort, the remnants of ring-forts which were small community settlements of the pre-Christian and early Christian periods. Again study the surrounding area and it will be clear that the monuments and cahers were focal points only of several acres of community structures.

Here in Ballynahown we find a number of wedge-monuments. Were they meditation centres, shepherd's huts or tombs? Nobody knows. Local legend has it that it was in one of these 'tombs' that Gráinne and her lover Diarmuid hid when they were fleeing from Finn MacCumhaill. Diarmuid covered the roof with seaweed so that when Finn consulted his oracle he only saw the seaweed and concluded they were drowned and gave up the chase leaving the lovers to besport themselves to their hearts' content.

You will now begin to notice the stone walls which abound in the Burren. Their construction was well thought out. They were loosely built so that the Atlantic gales could blow through them without knocking them and if an animal tried to knock one by pushing it the noise of the falling stones would frighten it so much that it would run away.

You can travel along this secret road and take a left turning on a byroad which twists and turns through delightful scenery and rejoins the main coast road. As you look towards the left you see the coast road to Ballyvaughan which is a most enchanting drive even if it is the tourist trail of the Burren.On one side is the Atlantic Ocean and the three Aran Islands. On the other side are all the varieties of the wild rugged Burren. Here we meet the real rocks that are 'His written word'. The road runs close to the sea and even the lightest summer breezes cause the waves to break splashing the foam high over the rocks. Standish O'Grady might well have been here when he wrote his beautiful poem *Foam Flakes*:

> Gotten in the strife of waters,
> Twinkling little stars of foam
> Restless beautiful white daughters
> Of a father made to roam.
>
> Fleeting shapes of rarest beauty
> Poetry and life and joy
> I would err in manhood's duty
> If I passed you like a boy.
>
> Forms as undefined as faces
> Seen in dreamland: ghosts of white
> Flowers that grew in heavenly places
> Fed on heavenly air and light.

Along this road one meets something we meet again and again in the Burren – the magical intriguing names which conjure up all kinds of mysterious nostalgia. How did they originate? Who baptised them? How long ago? We find Cloch Bharr an Choinín, the rock of the top of the rabbit; Leach na Naomh, the rock of the saints; Cloch an Oilc, the rock of the insult; and where the sea almost touches the road, Poll Máiréad Ní Thuathail, Margaret O'Toole's hole. I can imagine that not many people would like the latter address to head their notepaper!

The beautiful golden beach at Fanore is not one of the secret places of the Burren during the high summer season. Caravans, tents, transistors and plastic dominate the undulating sand hills. This can be annoying but these people too have a right to their own type of holiday and it is merely intolerant to sneer at them as if they were some kind of outcasts. Not everyone wants the secret places and those who do not are in no way inferior.

Usually in May or September, or very early in the morning one can find peace and quiet in Fanore. I can now recall many such moments of tranquillity when I stopped and took Maxie for a walk along the strand. Probably because his ancestors lived in a cold climate he does not like the heat, so he made his way into the water taking good care not to go too far out where the waves were breaking. There he lay down for a while looking happy and contented. Then he got up and rolled himself in the dry sand and then back again to the sea for another cool dip. So often we sat in the sand dunes enjoying the beauty of the restless, heaving sea but Fanore is always tinged with sadness for me as my memory slips back to the yesterdays when Mary was alive and we enjoyed ourselves with our children on this same beach. Now I was alone in the world and the hopes and dreams of those far off days were in ruins. Why is it that we humans only find out how deeply we love when that love is lost? It all happened so long ago and one should reasonably expect it to be forgotten, yet each time I come here one of those undimmed memories that are hidden deep in the mind jumps to the surface and implants its fierce stab of pain. I know it will always be so and it will happen again and again. Yet there is no remedy except to avoid self-pity and go right on.

They say however that tears are never very far away from laughter, and if this is so then laughter cannot be very far away from tears. Here in Fanore, while the sadness hurts deeply, it is tempered by the memory of laughter shared at a droll episode which took place here long years ago. Two nuns, carrying a large hold-all bag, came down to the strand, found a quiet hollow where they modestly undressed, put on the bathing suits, and went in for a swim. Two soldiers, who had obviously been discreetly observing and who were out for a bit of devilment, strolled over to where the nuns' clothes were. Unseen by the nuns the soldiers searched their hold-all and took out the nuns' camera. One of the soldiers dropped his trousers, exposed his genitals, while the other went down on one knee and took a photo of the object. He then wound on the camera, put it back in the nuns' bag, and both moved on. What happened when the film was developed? What did the local photographic shop think? If the Reverend Mother opened all letters coming into the convent what had she to say? And above all what did the two nuns think when they found such a strange picture among their snapshots? The charitable answer is, of course, that they did not know what it was a photograph of. So let us plump for charity and remember the words of Pope:

> In faith and hope the world will disagree
> But all mankind's concern is charity.

FOUR

ROADS OF SILENCE

Elected silence sing to me
And beat upon my whorléd ear
Pipe me to pastures still and be
The music that I care to hear.

GERARD MANLEY HOPKINS

The coast road winds around Black Head and into Ballyvaughan each mile revealing beauty after beauty. This is a tourist road for sightseers and photographers but it is well worth driving slowly along so that you can enjoy its splendid view of Galway Bay and the Connemara coast. Along this road, however, there are a few secret places where one can pause, rest and try to touch the infinite. Around Black Head itself you can search for the legendary caves where the banshee of the Burren, Bronach, lived long ago. When one of the O'Loughlins died Bronach set up a wail that, according to tradition, could be heard as far away as John B. Keane's pub in Listowel. Around here also, it is said, are hidden the fabulous treasures of the Fianna guarded, however, by the descendants of Bronach. If you search carefully you might find these treasures and make yourself a fortune, provided, of course, you can get past the weird sisters. Remember what happened to Macbeth after he dallied with the three apparitions. However, you never know your destiny and the best of Derrynaflan luck to you!

If you leave the main road a few hundred yards south of Black Head you will see a wall skirting the western side of the hill. Brace yourself for a good walk and follow this wall for about forty or forty-five minutes and you will come to the remains of a fort, Cathair Dhúin Irghuis. Irghuis was the son of a chieftain of the Burren, Huamore, and he was given Black Head Hill and fort as a wedding gift from his father – and what a delightful wedding gift it was! Irghuis built his caher here for his new bride and surrounded by this picturesque and romantic scenery, they began their young married life together. So sit down on the caher, take a rest and try to imagine what you would do with it if it were given to you as a wedding present.

If you continue along the wall for a distance of about two hundred and fifty yards and then turn to your right for about another two hundred and fifty yards and walk along the plateau you come to an incredible valley, reminiscent of the Grand Canyon, which separates Black Head from Aghaglinny. Close by is Carn Suí Finn. This is not just an ordinary heap of stones but, as you can see when you get near, a very skilfully constructed monument. According to tradition it was here Finn Mac Cumhaill held court when he visited this part of the Burren. Here he received gifts from local chieftains and, since he was not a marauder but a friend, the assembled company caroused, made merry and danced while his companions hunted the wolf, the stag and the wild boar around Black Head. In those days of long, sunny summers much jollification and high jinks took place in the open air. The women and men were so handsome and well-preserved that they did not need subdued lighting to hide the wrinkles on the face.

If you have a mind to, you can continue to the top of Black Head where there is another cairn called Dobhach Bhrainín, the Heap of Little Bran. One of Finn Mac-Cumhaill's famous wolfhounds was named Bran. It is possible that an offspring would have been called Braneen or Little Bran and it is also possible that Braneen could have been killed in the hunt and buried here. This would have been typical of the ancient Irish who loved their animals and it is much more likely to be the grave of a beloved dog than a grave of humans.

As you ramble up to the summit of Black Head the light may play strange tricks so that at times you feel as if the sunbeams themselves were lightly tripping along with you. At almost any point you can sit, relax and contemplate those great solitudes of beauty all around. It is such quiet moments that make the climb worth while. Resting here you may feel within yourself strange energies that shake the storehouse of memory, weave dreams in silence, and even bring you beyond the gates of death. The secret places of the Burren speak in their own hushed tones to the heart, and they speak differently to every one of us.

The coast road from Black Head to Ballyvaughan changes as one gets near the village. The landscape becomes a luxuriant green foliage which bursts forth along the lower perimeters of the hills highlighting the extraordinary contrast with the grey rock and green sea.

The village of Ballyvaughan, where for many years, I had a holiday cottage, has, in the intervening time, transformed itself almost beyond belief. It is now clean, tidy, tastefully adorned with excellent shops and cosy, intimate restaurants of character. Ballyvaughan was once O'Loughlin territory but in the sixteenth century it came into the possession of the O'Briens all because one of the O'Loughlins stole a

cow from the O'Briens who duly invaded and took possession of the whole of Ballyvaughan.

One of the saddest and most secret places is the ruins of
the old workhouse just on the outskirts of the village. Here
literally thousands of men, women and children starved to
death having been evicted by their Anglo-Irish landlords.
Describing one of these workhouses a sincere British army
officer, Captain Kennedy, wrote:

We admitted a considerable number of paupers among whom
were some of the most appalling cases of destitution and suffering
it has ever been my lot to witness. The state of most of these
wretched creatures is traceable to the numerous evictions which
have taken place. When driven from their cabins they betake
themselves to the ditches and there exist like animals. . . there
were three cartloads of these creatures brought for admission
yesterday, some in fever, some from dysentery and all from want
of food. . . There were days when I came back from some scene
of eviction so maddened by the sights of hunger and misery I
had seen in the day's work that I felt disposed to take a gun and
shoot the first landlord I met.

The landlords are now gone. The people of Clare rose in
arms and by a combination of bullet and ballot banished
them. The crumbling ruins of Ballyvaughan workhouse
eloquently symbolise the ruin of the evil empire which
inflicted such cruelties and barbarities.

If instead of going straight on at Fanore you turn to the
right, through what is known as the Khyber Pass, you enter
one of the most secret places of the Burren, the Caher river
valley, full of surprises. The Caher river itself is one of those
surprises. It is the only river in this area that flows above
ground all the way. The reason for this is unknown. It
patters its way, twists and turns, dances and leaps, especially if swollen by rain, all down the valley. Finally, just as

it is about to enter the Atlantic, it disappears as if it wanted to tell us that it is master of its own destiny.

The Caher valley is a haven for the contemplative seeking an answer to the riddle of life or for whispering lovers wondering if what they now feel will last for all time.

About a mile and a half along this valley road having crossed a bridge – stop to see what is called Fualacht Fiadh which is translated as 'cooking place' although I do not know why. Fiadh means 'deer' or 'wild' and Fualacht means something to do with urine so 'pissy deer' would be a literal translation. Surely there is something wrong here. It is of course quite possible that 'Fualacht' is a corruption of 'folcha' which means a bath. If this were the case it could be translated as 'bath in the wild'. This field monument is a small horseshoe shaped mound near the river and is said, by the scholars, to be an ancient cooking place for hunting parties. According to this theory a wooden trough was constructed and filled with water. Then a fire was started nearby in which large stones were heated. These stones in turn were then dropped into the filled trough and the water would boil in half an hour. Legs of mutton and sides of pork thatched with straw, were, it is said, cooked in the boiling water. I must admit that it works. I tried it once with the late Professor M. J. O'Kelly at a site in County Cork – and the mutton tasted superb.

Nevertheless I am not fully convinced that they were cooking places. It was Geoffrey Keating who first put forward this explanation in the seventeenth century and Keating was a notoriously naive historian. The concept of going to all this trouble does not seem to me to make sense. They could so easily have cooked the meat on a spit, or indeed on the stones themselves. I am inclined to the view that these monuments had nothing to do with cooking but were in fact hot baths. They were usually found in groups of six or seven. This would indicate one per family and it seems unlikely they were constructed by nomads. The heat of the water could easily be regulated by the number of stones put in and the whole thing could be every bit as good as the hot springs of Iceland or New Zealand.

In an old manuscript copied in 1629 by Michael O'Cleary, one of the Four Masters, there is an account of St Berach who was told by his Abbot to prepare water to wash the feet of some monks due to arrive in the monastery after a long and tiresome journey. He put one stone for every monk in the fire and as each one was ready to wash he put a stone in the 'Fualacht Fiadh'. There is no mention of it being used for cooking. There is also evidence that close to the trough there was a kind of wattle hut – something like a wigwam. This could have been used either as a dressing and drying room or as a sauna heated also by hot stones. The scholars, however, tell us they were used for cooking and scholars are knowledgeable people. Some of them told us years back that there were no 'Fualacht Fiadh' west of the Shannon. Since that statement scores have been found in Clare alone. Anyway the 'Fualacht Fiadh' are one more Burren mystery to whet the appetite and confound the learned.

About another half a mile along this road on the left-hand side and about a hundred yards up a slope there is a dense growth of scrub which hides the little penal chapel of Fermoyle. This little chapel is only about six yards square with a rather crude stone in the centre, which was probably used as an altar. Sometimes the persecution by the British occupational forces during the penal days has been compared to the persecution of Jews by the Nazis in occupied countries. The savagery inflicted on the priests and people in the penal days is paralleled only by the later atrocities of Hitler. Men, women and children were murdered without mercy. Indeed some units of the British army specialised in carrying screaming infants around on top of their spears. White in his *History of Clare* gives one particular incident of this brutality:

Priests and religious were so persecuted in those years in Clare, that some of them, losing courage, petitioned for a vessel to take them to some other country. Their request was granted. A vessel called at Scattery to take them on board, but when well out at sea, all of them, numbering forty-six, were plunged overboard.

In another frightening passage White describes the death of one Irishman at the hands of Sir John Perrott:

He had him first half-hanged from the shafts of a car. Then his bones were broken by strokes of a heavy axe, and his mangled body, while he was still alive, was fastened with ropes to the top of the tower of Quin Abbey, as a feast for the birds of the air.

Thousands of such incidents are recorded and the mind simply flounders at the thought of human beings sinking so low – and there were no Nuremburg trials to punish them. But the little penal church in Fermoyle, and so many other similar ruins will always be there to remind us of the harsh and bitter truth.

This simple church was only one of hundreds scattered throughout the country. It was well concealed by bush and scrub from the British mercenaries and priest-hunters. Look-outs were posted at vantage points and the people cautiously gathered there on Sundays to pray knowing that execution awaited them if they were caught. Every time I visit it I feel impelled to bend in reverence and kiss the little altar. The sense of tragedy which envelops the place turns to pride and joy when I recall that I am one of this race who could not be conquered or subdued. Kissing that old crude stone is, for me, a greater experience than kissing a Papal ring amid all the splendours and glories of the Vatican.

Turn left just a short distance up the road and follow a steep bohereen into a farmyard. From there you can walk up a slope to the deserted village of Caherbeannagh, in translation The Fox's Den. If ever human beings evicted foxes from here, then the foxes have won the final battle. A sad scene of several houses in ruins – a whole village gone. It is only one of several such villages in the Burren. Where? When? How? It is impossible to walk amongst these ruins without feeling at one with the people – with their misfortune, their anguish, their pain, without even dying their deaths. The rot started in the aftermath of the Great Famine of which George Bernard Shaw said: 'When a country is full of food and exporting it there can be no famine.' Shaw is suggesting here that the Famine was deliberate genocide to exterminate the Irish race.

There is much evidence to show that it was. Nassau Senior, one of the British government's advisors on economic affairs, said that the Famine in Ireland would not kill more than a million people and that would scarcely be enough to do much good. He was hoping for much more devastation and he got it.

Pádraig Pearse commented:

The British never commit a useless crime. When they hire a man to assassinate an Irish patriot, when they blow a sepoy [an Indian] from the mouth of a cannon, when they produce a famine in one of their dependencies, they have always an ulterior motive. . . Every crime the English have planned and carried out in Ireland has had a definite end.

In 1841 there was a population in Clare of 286,394. By the time the Famine ended it had been reduced to half that figure. There was plenty of grain but the landlords seized it for rent and exported it. There are several tragic cases of a boatload of Irish grain leaving Irish harbours and meeting a boatload of grain as relief from British Quakers coming in. The human suffering in Clare was beyond belief. A Captain Wynne writes:

I confess myself shocked by the extent and intensity of the suffering I witnessed, more especially among the women and little children, crowds of whom were to be seen scattered over the turnip fields. . . devouring the raw turnips, mothers half-naked, shivering in the snow and sleet, uttering exclamations of despair whilst their children were screaming with hunger.

What Wynne saw could be multiplied to cover every village in Ireland. Hundreds of thousands dying on roadsides, in fields and in the ditches. It was a famine that need never have had such disastrous results – the virtual strangulation to death of millions of helpless people in a few short years. . . Hitler believed that the slaughter of millions of Jews was a 'final solution'. Stalin thought that the murder of three million Ukranians was also a final solution. Did Britain believe that the elimination of four million Irish would be a final solution too? Yet the Jews survived, the Ukranians survived, the Irish survived and their executioners are gone. Britain has lost her empire, and in world affairs she no longer has influence, she has only an opinion. Her faithful servants are gone too. Lord Brougham, who said 'It was the landlord's right to do as he pleased; the tenants must be taught by the strong arm of the law that they had no power to oppose or resist' is gone too. So is Lord Macaulay who asked, 'How do you govern Ireland? Not by love but by fear. . . by means of armed men and entrenched camps.'

Little wonder that the unknown Irish poet who saw the corpse of an Englishman hanging from a tree could write:

Good is thy fruit O tree!
The bulk of thy fruit on every bough!
Would that the trees of Ireland
Were full of thy fruit every day!

But the Irish spirit endured and they went on to rebel
again and again until they finally drove the invaders from
most of their country.

The last time I was in the lonesome deserted village of
Caherbeannagh I could only bow my head in silent sorrow-
ful prayer for those who had made it possible for me to live
as a free man. But it is always a sad, painful experience to
relive the past amid the ruins of these little homes.

Having driven along this delightful valley for another
mile or so I parked the car in a little opening near the Green
Road and went for a walk with Maxie. It was a day for
strolling rather than driving. The beauty surrounding me
on all sides helped to banish some of the sad thoughts that
occupied my mind. We were alone and we sauntered along
the road together. Our only companions were the wonderful Burren flora in full bloom, the birds singing in the hazel
trees, the uncertain hum of the wandering bees. Here was
a secret spring of beauty. We are forever searching for the
spot where the rainbow hides, I thought, and if it hides
anywhere it must be surely here.

We swung along slowly until we came to a little field and
there we met our first fellow being – a donkey. He was
standing gazing in the direction of the strange wild light
shimmering on the mountain tops, like a Tibetan mystic at
prayer. When I scratched his forehead he responded grate-
fully. Maxie did not even bark at him but just sniffed around
to ensure there was no danger. The cross on the donkey's
back was clearly visible. The Gospels tell that Christ rode

into Jerusalem on a donkey on Palm Sunday and ever since there is the outline of a cross on his back. The great English writer and poet G. K. Chesterton used that event to immortalise the donkey in his famous poem:

When fishes flew and forests walked
And figs grew upon a thorn
Some moment when the moon was blood
Then surely I was born.

With monstrous head and sickening cry
And ears like errant wings
The devil's walking parody
On all four-footed things.

The tattered outlaw of the earth,
Of ancient crooked will,
Starve, scourge, deride me: I am dumb,
I keep my secret still,

Fools! for I also had my hour,
One far fierce hour and sweet;
There was a shout about my ears,
And palms before my feet.

Chesterton was one of a gifted band of British writers like Hilaire Belloc, Thomas Paine, William Cobbett, George Orwell and Claude Cockburn who dedicated their lives to the promulgation of truth and who refused to be bribed by the establishment into the acceptance of injustice. For this reason they were all friends of Ireland and their efforts go a long way towards blotting out the bitterness felt by the Irish people for the British establishment.

In one delightful stanza Chesterton whimsically shows that he had a deep understanding of the Irish people:

> The great men of Ireland
> The men whom God made mad
> Whose wars are always merry
> But whose songs are always sad.

When he came to Ireland during the Eucharistic Congress he was deeply impressed, not by the pomp and triumphalism, but by a banner he saw across Dominick Street in Dublin. The banner read: GOD BLESS THE SACRED HEART. The theology might be somewhat off-beat but the sentiments were in the right place.

The Green Road along here becomes a bohereen and is beautiful in its loneliness. It is not very well kept, but that only adds to its charm. It is the kind of road that invites you along. Even though it is long and straight it undulates up and down as if to relieve tiredness. It is now much the same as it was a thousand years ago when it linked up Corker Pass, Corcomroe Abbey, Caher Valley, Ballinlacken and perhaps Kilfenora and Limerick. Along the sides of this road and in the adjoining fields you can see the Alpine and Mediterranean flora best. Here too you may run into a herd of wild goats, valued by the farmers as the most efficient of weed killers. Here too if you are observant you may meet the shy pine-marten, the badger, the stoat and indeed the mink. The Green Road and the barren rugged landscape around it is a little paradise, a delightful secret spot to sit and rest and think.

There are several little side trips which can be made in this area. If you take the road from Fermoyle to Caheranardurrish you will pass the ruins of an old chapel which was once a famous shebeen. What a delightful place to have an illegal pub. Further on that road a right turn will bring you back to the main Lisdoonvarna road but on the way you pass to your left a cluster of interesting forts: Lismacsheedy, Lisnagat, Lismacteigue. On the other side of the road a visit to Rathborney Church is well worth-while. This church was built on an old ring fort and has a most interesting window and holy water font. If you examine your map carefully you will find all kinds of secret roadways and pathways here, each one of them full of beauty and mystery and well worth exploring.

On the main road back towards Lisdoonvarna you pass on your right-hand side the entrance to one of the most famous Burren caves, Poll na gColm, the Opening of the Doves.

The caves are the most secret of all places in the Burren. But a word of warning must be sounded here. These caves are only for the experienced. It is highly dangerous to attempt to negotiate them except in the company of an experienced spelaeologist. They are very much subject to change in weather and sometimes after rain the caverns get flooded, escape becomes impossible and a horrible death dangerously close. Large sections of the caves have to be explored on hands and knees and when these extremely low passages begin to flood then the situation becomes really perilous and the danger to life is really acute.

The first recorded account we have of cave exploration in the Burren comes from Dr Charles Lucas in 1736, and since then brave men and women have risked their lives in these unknown regions to add to our knowledge of this mysterious landscape. Indeed in almost every decade new caves and passages are being discovered so that by now close on one hundred miles of dark underground passageways have been explored. For those who would like to know more about this daring and unusual pastime I can heartily recommend that wonderful book *The Caves of North-West Clare* edited by E. K. Tratman.

Many of the caves, however, were used from a very early

age. Animal bones, and indeed human bones, have been found from time to time, and no doubt those caves that were big enough and of easy access served to house domestic animals or as temporary dwellings. But above all they were used as hiding places, caverns of refuge particularly when the Danes were marauding and later when the British were ravaging the land.

One other use which they were inevitably put to was to house illicit poteen-stills. They gave perfect cover and protection from the police who prudently avoided any chase into such dangerous lairs. I was told a delightful story of one such still which was operated at the turn of the century by an old expert whom we shall call Johnny, although that was not his real name.

Johnny and his family had been making poteen for generations and despite every effort, and indeed some raids, they had successfully eluded the Royal Irish Constabulary, as the police were then called. For the last Christmas of the century Johnny anticipated there would be extra celebrations and merriment to see the year out so he busied himself early on to make sure he could meet the demand. The police anticipated that some such activities might be afoot, and so, shortly before the festive season, they made a dawn swoop on Johnny's still, but despite the most extensive search not a drop of poteen could be found. They did however find his illegal equipment and he was duly charged before the next court.

The magistrate, a pompous individual, delivered a long tirade against Johnny saying that if even one drop of poteen had been found Johnny would spend the next couple of Christmases in jail. As he was only found with the equipment, the magistrate concluded, the maximum he could do was to fine Johnny £10. Johnny quickly whipped out two £10 notes out of his back pocket, laid them on the bench, and made to leave the courtroom. As he reached the door the magistrate called after him: 'What are the two £10 notes for? I only fined you one £10.'

'Your worship,' said Johnny, 'the second one is for the rape.'

'What rape?' queried the magistrate, 'you were not charged with any rape here today.'

'I know,' quipped Johnny. 'But amn't I in possession of the equipment for same?' And he was out of the door that instant.

Be that as it may, as the old storyteller would say, the caves of the Burren are not to be trifled with. There is however one cave which should not be missed and that is the Aillwee Cave, near Ballyvaughan. This cave has been developed especially for visitors. A flagged path has been laid down and electric lighting installed. Guided tours take place at regular intervals during the summer. At the entrance to the cave there is a charming restaurant and craft shop, and an excellent selection of Irish books. Do not forget to pause a moment outside in the car park. The view is simply superb.

If you continue on towards Lisdoonvarna you pass through Toomaghera, now a peaceful little village, but in 1831 the scene of a most terrible massacre. This time it was not the British killing the Irish but the Irish killing the British. Five policemen, servants of the crown, had arrested Tom McInerney, a blacksmith for seditious offences, and almost the entire adult population of the village unarmed surrounded the police and demanded the release of McInerney. The police refused and as if to make an example they fired at one man in the crowd named Hoare and riddled his body with bullets. Enraged by this act the villagers turned on the police and beat them to death leaving not one of them alive. Those they did not beat they shot with captured police guns.

There were no witnesses prepared to come forward and give evidence, so the state took one at random, John O'Grady, tried him on false evidence and hanged him in Toomaghera. Such was British justice long before the Birmingham and Guildford bombings.

Just beyond Toomaghera turn up a little byroad to look at the ruins of the fourteenth century church of Kilmoon which is now disgracefully allowed to fall into almost complete decay. I have searched many times for the grave of Hoare who was shot by the police that terrible day in Toomaghera but I could not find it. Almost every grave is overgrown. Nearby is St Mogua's well and close by is a set of cursing stones.

These cursing stones are a feature of the Burren. Just off the road from Carron to Bell Harbour is Bearna na Mallacht, the Cursing Gap, at one time a great centre for avenging your wrongs. Again at the cave of St Colman Mac Duagh there are several of these stones. Why should they be found in such holy places? The procedure for cursing your neighbour was to go there fasting and do seven rounds of the stones against the sun, turn each stone in the direction of where you think your victim is, hop once on each leg and say: 'May the seven sows of hell move their bowels on his breast and curse him to damnation.' There is, in fact, a record from the early years of this century of a court case where a farmer was prosecuted for beating a beggar woman. His defence was that she threatened 'to turn the stones of Kilmoon against him'.

I once had a friend, a distinguished scholar, who turned the stones and seriously cursed a colleague. Sadly the colleague was killed shortly afterwards and my friend was obsessed with a deep remorse until the day he died. But these stones have their comic element. An old man told me that as a child he saw crowds coming there, cursing their neighbours on the stones, and then saying the rosary and making offerings at the well. The inconsistency did not worry him. 'Sure God was a carpenter,' he said, 'and he should known the mind of the people. If he had a spark of commonsense he'd understand.'

A short distance before you come to the famous Corkscrew hill on the Lisdoonvarna side there is a little byroad to the right which leads to Cahermacnaughten which is one of the best known early Irish ring forts and it has an added interest in that it was adapted and enlarged to become a very famous Irish law school run by the O'Davoren family. Apart from just teaching law to students from various tribes these law schools performed a very valuable judicial function in so far as the head of the school was entitled to sign legal documents. Without his signature the document was not valid. What a wise precaution that was! It meant that one party to an agreement could not easily pull the wool over the eyes of the second party. The eagle eye of the law school head would be sure to detect any trickery.

One of the greatest Irish scholars of the century, Duald Mac Firbis, taught here. He was the compiler of probably the most valuable Irish historical book *Pedigrees of Ancient Irish families*. He moved from one academic destinction to another and lived to the ripe old age of eighty. He was murdered in the village of Dunflin in Sligo. While Duald was resting in an inn an Englishman named Crofton made advances towards the barmaid who called out to him for help. In a rage Crofton took up a carving knife from the table and plunged it into Mac Firbis' heart. That was the end of the matter. Crofton, being an Englishman, was never put on trial.

The code of law studied at this great school was of course,

the Brehon Laws, far wiser and far more humane than Roman or English law which is the basis of our present code. Today there is widespread controversy and discussion on hot-line subjects of marriage, divorce and the rights of women. Two thousand years ago the Brehon Laws showed rationality, good judgment and clear thinking in these important matters.

These laws for example, were explicit on the type of man that could *not* contract marriage: 1) A barren man 2) An unarmed man (isn't that a delightful way to describe impotence?) 3) A man in Holy Orders 4) A rockman, that is a man without arable land 5) An obese man – obviously because he might not be able to perform even with the best will in the world 6) A claenán, that is a man likely to gossip about his wife's performance in bed.

In the Brehon Laws there was no such thing as an illegitimate child. All children born to woman, whether married or single, had equal rights. There were however some obligations on the mother. A child born of a man who had been forbidden to marry must be maintained by the mother. The child of a harlot or that of a carnal tourist, the child of a man in Holy Orders, the child of an outcast – all had to be supported by the mother. Other than these exceptions the happy fathers had to support their children and almost invariably the word of the mother prevailed.

The case of the husband who decided to have a little flutter on the quiet was also prudently provided for. The woman had the final say in the matter. She could kill her female rival, but wisely, not until three days after the event. She could also do likewise to her husband. Imagine the problems that could cause today!

Divorce was allowed in the case of serious illness, long term absence, incurable injury, insanity, one party barren, slander, violence which leaves a mark, impotence, refusal of conjugal rights, failure to provide a home and board. It is important to remember that mere incompatability in itself was not grounds for divorce.

The family was the basic unit and even though a man might have many wives all had specific legal rights. There were also varying degrees of status dependent not only on birth but also on economic standing and learning. Farming was to a large extent co-operative and the family were responsible for debts – so a watchful eye was kept on the wayward son or daughter. In the Brehon Laws you were entitled to hospitality when making a journey. You could, however, only claim from one higher in status than your-self. This wise law meant that the rich could not abuse the poor. Furthermore all you could claim was milk, cheese and bread – no butter, meat or booze.

Perhaps the most intriguing section of the Brehon Laws concerns sexual crimes. In his scolarly and most readable paperback, *Sex and Marriage in Ancient Ireland* Dr Patrick C. Power lists a few of these:

1. If a man's penis is cut off the wretched sufferer is entitled to two kinds of compensation for his loss. Naturally his full honour-price had to be paid and in addition to this the atonement called *corp-dire* in full. . .

2. The case of him whose scrotum is cut off comes next. For some odd reason only the *corp-dire* is payable in this case. . .

3. The tract then discusses the fellow whose left testicle only is removed. For this deed the penalty was full body price of *corp-dire*. The reason for this had its roots in mediaeval theory. It was thought that the left testicle was the active agent in procreation and they evidently regarded the companion as a balancing ornament.

4. As might be anticipated the removal of the right testicle earned a penalty which was equal to part of the body price only.

5. The final detail is that a much diminished penalty for full castration is payable to a man in Holy Orders or a decrepit old fellow. Reasonably enough it is stated that such a person had no need for his generative organs.

In a telling passage Dr Power writes:

Looking back to the 1920s it is a little strange that the first native government took over the full British system of law virtually without a single alteration. No attempt whatever was made to form a native system. When one looks at the declared aims of this and later governments to Gaelicise the country, one can only comment on the shallow hypocrisy of it all.

Standing on top of the stony old mound at Cahermacnaughten and surveying the landscape and the distant sea one can visualise it as it was – the wattle huts of the professors, the lecture halls, the extensive library, the several craft shops, the grianán for the ladies to chat and embroider, the scores of other buildings to support the school – it must have been an inspiring sight. But the British destroyed it all in the seventeenth century and burned to ashes the priceless manuscripts and library. Today it is just a mound of memories.

A turning to the left just beyond Cahermacnaughten leads to the twelfth century church of Noughaval. At the entrance to the church there is a market-cross pedestal — but the cross is missing. These monuments were used for measuring cloth, timber, etc, on market days. The stone would have been surmounted by a cross – presumably the cross might inspire a spot of honesty in the dealers.

The ruined church itself is a delightful, peaceful, secret place. By standing on the wall and looking around the surroundings one can visualise this small monastic settlement, perhaps with only a few monks living in their wattle huts, and ministering to the needs of the people and presumably

Trumpeter on grave-slab, Noughaval

the needs of the law students at nearby Cahermacnaughten. Noughaval, like many other small churches is a
place of prayer and meditation – a place where one can feel
the presence of God in every stone. In the churchyard itself
there are scores of graves, including a special vault of the
O'Davorens of the law school. Although this was not built
until 1725 local tradition says that it was the burial place of
the professors of the law school for centuries. A particularly
interesting grave is that of one of the Keane family who
died in 1799. It is a flat slab with several delightful inscrip-
tions, including the sun, moon, thirty pieces of silver, cock
crowing and many others. In another corner is an interesting celtic cross only a few feet high. It is very hard to date
it but it must surely be at least a thousand years old. Whose
remains lie underneath?

The old Irish chieftains loved their graves. They had a
healthy outlook on death. One of them, Art Aenfhir wrote:

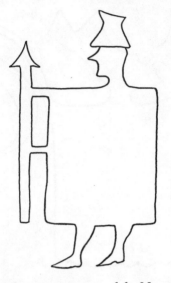

Lance-bearer on grave-slab, Noughaval

My mound! My protection after parting with my army,
My pure bright haven, my tomb, my grave!

Many times I have sat beside this historic cross and fell to wondering what it must be like to be dead a thousand years.

Death and graveyards have always had a peculiar fascination for me. I have never been able to accept that death is the end. And if it is not the end then surely it must be the beginning. There is more scientific evidence for this than for the opposite theory. We all at different times of our life experience the eternal: the moment of first love, the awakening to a creative idea, the song of the lark, the innocence of a child, the heart of a rose, the sheer joy of being alive. But those beautiful moments pass. 'Stay O Happy Moment Stay!' was the agonising cry of Faust. But they do not stay because our existence is ruled by Time. But the dead are

outside Time. They know the answers to every baffling question; they know the last unwritten and revealing chapter in the book of life. Compared to us they are so far superior in beauty and intelligence as to defy understanding by the human brain. The love which they bear to one another is a completely purified form of love, devoid of all selfishness and possessiveness; it is a burning flame millions of times more intense than ever earthly love could be. I doubt very much if we can be of any help to them – but they can certainly help us – which is why I always feel inclined to pray *to* the dead not *for* them. Well might the poet ponder:

> Our birth is but a sleep and a forgetting
> The soul that rises with us, our life's star
>   Hath had elsewhere its setting
>   And cometh from afar
>   Not in entire forgetfulness
>   And not in utter nakedness
> But trailing clouds of glory do we come
> From God who is our home.

Noughaval is a place of meditation and prayer – a place where one renews the spirit – a place where one can experience moments of great beauty that time could never lessen and where, as one leaves, it is as if you were bringing some of its eternal life with you.

It is only when you stand amid the ruins of such places as Kilmoon and Fermoyle, Cahermacnaughten and Kilnaboy that you realise how disgracefully we treat our national shrines – for that is what they are. We allow them to fall into decay, to become lost in the undergrowth and we do not really seem to care. Is it that our rulers and civil servants are secretly ashamed of their past now that they have their Mercedes and massive pensions to console them? Is it that they lack even the rudiments of vision and farsightedness? Is it no little wonder that so many foreign visitors regard us as a truly retarded, backward race. The restoration of places like Holycross, Craganowen, gives a ray of hope. Perhaps those who regard themselves as our superiors might carefully ponder the words of that great Irishman, Father MacDyer:

There is a famine abroad – a famine not of bread nor of gold, but a famine of really great men. We are stained with mediocrity, we are dying of ordinariness, we are perishing of pettiness.

The state of the great monastic sites of Ireland bear witness to that comment.

Angel on tombstone, Noughaval

102

FIVE

THE VALLEY OF
THE FERTILE ROCK

*Man! Can'st thou build upon ought in
    the pride of thy mind
Wisdom will teach thee that nothing can
    tarry behind.
Though there be a thousand bright
    actions embalmed and enshrined
Myriads and millions of brighter are
    snow in the wind.*

JAMES CLARENCE MANGAN

The road from Noughaval to Carron is another of the Burren's secret roads, full of twists and turns, meandering through a variety of contrasting landscapes, reminding one at times of an Alpine ski-track – and every few miles along the way there is a monument of some kind to be visited and explored.

Less than a mile out of Carron on the Bell Harbour road there is a little bohereen to the right. Take this bohereen almost as far as you can go to a townland called Termon and then walk across a field to the right to Temple Cronan,

Temple Cronan

which for me is the crown jewel, the priceless pearl, the most secret place in the Burren.

Temple Cronan is just a little paradise. It is almost as old as Irish Christianity itself. It was founded in the sixth century by St Cronan. It was said that some years after its foundation Cronan felt it was too isolated to minister to the needs of the people so he transferred to Roscrea, which was then on one of the main trans-country highways, and there founded a much larger monastery. He took some of the monks with him to Roscrea and left a few others behind to continue the settlement here in Termon. I have little doubt had I been one of those monks I would have opted to stay here. It is a small church with all the signs of ancient Irish Christianity – the few carvings protruding from the west gable are so old as to be almost indecipherable.

The boundary wall surrounding the churchyard is in the form of a triangle. In one corner there is a reliquary built

of large flagstones so placed as to meet at the top like the roof of a church or an elongated pyramid. This originally contained relics, usually the bones of a saint, which the public could touch by putting their hands in through a small hole in one end. Unfortunately this end is missing but I have seen a perfect one, complete with hole, at Kilbounia near Cahirciveen. Outside the boundary wall to the north are the remains of a pedestal of a high cross, and to the south a holy well.

It is not too hard to imagine what Temple Cronan was like in its hey-day. It was, of course, not a great monastery like Kilfenora or Corcomroe. It was one of those small secluded centres of prayer that are found in so many parts of Ireland. Temple Cronan probably never had more than half-a dozen or ten monks. It would have been surrounded by a strong circular wall, of about five hundred yards diameter, to protect it from wild animals and particularly wolves, which roamed the Burren freely in those days. The church would be the central building, and close-by a kitchen, refectory, and the wattle huts of the monks. These huts were made of wattles, were thatched and quite comfortable. They were so constructed as to contain a small fire in real cold weather. Within the outer wall of the settlement there would have been a pastoral area for cattle, sheep, hens and bees and again a tilled area for root crops, vegetables and corn. It would be a self-sufficient small community. I strongly suspect that the field on the north side was a beautiful terraced garden of flowers, shrubs and trees. All in all it would have been a place of domestic beauty and tranquillity.

The isolated and primitive nature of Temple Cronan prompts an incisive question that has been asked again and again for hundreds of years: What was it that inspired sane, intelligent men and women to leave their homes, families,

friends and to renounce the possibility of a loving companion and children of their own, for such a life of austerity?

It was a question that intrigued me very much until, by good fortune, I came to know two such men. One was a brilliant nuclear physicist and the other a distinguished doctor. Both were in their early thirties, unmarried, and both joined enclosed contemplative orders. They both honoured me with their confidences and so I gradually came to a deeper understanding, not only of what motivated them personally, but of a better appreciation of the very meaning of life itself.

Everything flowed from one basic philosophy: *The human being exists solely for the purpose of becoming an earthly life-form of God*. Man was the earthly individualisation of God, there was no man *and* God. There was only man *as* God. The inner dimension in man should rule his life, and that inner dimension was God. Everything else was a mere side show. One lived then a life in practical terms in as close a union as possible with God. One did not do it for a reward. One did it because this is the only rational explanation of life itself, the only explanation that gives meaning to death.

The average person on the outside would be inclined to feel that if you take away sex, money, power and success from life you are left with nothing, and there is little point in staying alive. The monk sees it differently. All these things are to him transient. As soon as you achieve one you want more and more and each achievement becomes emptier and shallower and brings on more and more stress and tension. The highly successful man in material terms may well be the unhappiest. The rate of suicide amongst them is very high, if not the highest.

According to the monks the best things in life are those which come from within: creativity, tolerance, living in the present, meditation, contemplation and above all a loving

care for all life, not just human beings, but every living thing. A life lived in those terms brought unbelievable happiness, they said. I remember well an analogy one of them made: a stained glass window looked at from the outside is merely a grayish glaze. But looked at from the inside it is a thing of indescribable beauty. If you are on the inside you can experience everything to its fullest. If we accept the 'inner' life it does not really matter whether or not we are in a monastery – fulfilment of life's purpose will be ours.

Both of these man are now dead. One gave up world-wide fame, the other gave up possibly becoming very wealthy. Neither of them would concede that they 'gave up' anything. They would contend that they merely gave up trash for happiness. Indeed both were two of the happiest men I ever knew.

The monks who lived here in Temple Cronan could be said to be of the same mould. The conditions under which they lived may well frighten us – the cold, the heat, the spartan living, the doubts, the dark night of the soul – but they did not see it so! The eternal love which motivated my friends was the same love which motivated the monks of more than a thousand years ago. 'Seek ye first the Kingdom of Heaven and all other things will be added to you.' If you ask: Where do I find the Kingdom of Heaven? the voice may come across the centuries and tell you: 'The Kingdom of Heaven is within you.' If we take it a step further, heed this voice and perfect that which is within us namely, the mind and the soul, it may not be long before we are jumping and shouting with joy like the blind man in the Gospel: 'I was blind. Now I see.'

Whenever I visit the Burren I usually manage to spend a few hours in Temple Cronan. Here I can stretch out on the grass and lose myself in contemplation in the company of the unseen men of holiness who are dead more than a thousand years. With them I try to see the hand of God in the beauties of nature all around, the rolling clouds, the soft west wind, the singing of the birds and the distant call of the sea. Like Wordsworth, one can touch the essence of being:

> . . . and I have felt
> A presence that disturbs me with the joy
> Of elevated thoughts; a sense sublime
> Of something far more deeply interfused
> Whose dwelling is the light of setting suns
> And the round ocean and the living air
> And the blue sky and in the mind of men
> A motion and a spirit that impels
> And thinning things, all objects of all thought
> And rolls through all things.

As you walk slowly away from this prayerful place you will find it hard to realise that there exists in the same country crime, torture, injustice, income tax, insurance claims, unemployment, computers and all the other paraphernalia that contribute so much to our discontent. In Temple Cronan it all seems so far, far away. But Temple Cronan is not a place for self-pity. It should inspire as well a little of the spirit of the men who lived there long ago.

Come back to the village of Carron and take a left turn and just past the Galway University field research station bear left towards the Burren perfumery. Not far along this road you will see again on your left just inside the ditch a cross and a number of boulder stones. This is often called St Fachtna's Well, but this is a bit puzzling. St Fachtna had nothing to do with Clare – indeed he was a good strong West Cork man from Roscarbery. The map calls it Tobar

na Fiaghanta, which would mean the Well of the Rushes –
a much more likely name. The old Irish were great for tack-
ing on the name of the saint to a place in order to give it
that extra bit of a fillup. The resemblance between Fachtna
and Fiaghanta is not too far removed and anyway poor
Fachtna would hardly have objected.

If you have by any chance misbehaved yourself the night
before in Lisdoonvarna, and if your head is not feeling as
clear as it should, then here is a chance to make amends.
Go to each of the boulders in turn, say three Hail Marys,
hop twice on each leg and, they say, you have a fair chance
of having your head cured and your misdemeanours over-
looked. The last time I visited here in a fit of piety I started
to do the rounds but Maxie took the edge off me by proceed-
ing ahead and putting the stones to a use for which they
were never intended. I gave up and let nature run its course.

As you continue your journey along this road which
twists and turns, rises and falls, you are really in another
secret place of the Burren. Sometimes you drive through a
glacial valley, hemmed in on all sides, other times the hazel
seems to close around you like a tunnel of trees, other times
there is nothing around you but the bare desolate landscape
of the Burren. On this road I have often had the feeling
that the landscape itself was in some way alive and moving.
Was it possible that some power in my mind had tuned
into the rotation of the earth?

Further along this road at a place called Keelhilla we run
into the traces of a very colourful gentleman named St Colman Mac Duagh. You will have to park the car and take a
little trip across country. There is the makings of a novel
in his story which was told to me in a pub in Lisdoonvarna
by a wizened little old man with the clear, honest face of
an accomplished liar.

'St Colman MacDuagh,' he explained, 'got his schoolin''

beyond in Aran. The master was St Enda, a fairly tough customer who was a bit of a playboy when he was young and who was frightened into becoming a saint when he saw the dead body of one of his tally-women who threw herself out of a window after a night of drunken divarsion. Anyway, when St Colman was able to read and write and do a few sums Enda sent him to Keelhilla to do penance for seven years. He was only allowed to have one servant, a poor simpleton. The two of them spent the years there in a cave doin' penance and prayin'. One Easter Sunday they were starving with the hunger and the poor simpleton said how much he would like to have his snout stuck in a feed of pig's head and cabbage. At that moment King Guaire in Kinvara was sitting down to his dinner of pig's head and cabbage when all of a sudden the plates left the table, and flew out the window carrying all the food. King Guaire and his followers chased the plates on horseback and kept after them 'till they got to Keelhilla. When they crossed the field there they found Colman and the simpleton layin' into the pig's head, cabbage and wine. The poor simpleton was so hungry that he ate plate and all and was choked on the spot. They waked him that night and buried him dacent in the morning and you can see his grave there to this very day. You can also see the tracks of King Guaire's horses all along the rocks of the Burren. It is now called Bothar na Mias – the Road of the Dishes. The King took a likin' to St Colman and offered to build him a decent church somewhere not so far away from the public. He told St Colman to keep walkin' and when his belt fell off of him the church would be built on that spot. Poor Colman started off on foot followed by Guaire and his men on horseback. They travelled all day and the belt stayed where it was. They were outside Gort when St Colman got short-taken' and whilst he was relieving himself behind a furze bush by God, didn't the belt fall to the ground. 'Twas loosened, you know, on account of the little job he was at – so on that very spot King Guaire built a grand big cathedral and a round tower, made Colman a bishop for life and called the place Kilmacduagh. The fellow that built the round tower was a Connemara man who was drunk most of the time for it is leanin' to one side like that other tower in Italy, the pissin' tower or some quare name like that.'

The old man told me that story without even the sign of a smirk on his face and it was well worth the couple of pints it cost me. It would be unkind to say that he told me lies. Rather would I prefer to say that he exaggerated the truth.

But of course the truth can be relative and very elusive. Our modern world is inclined to sneer at such strange happenings but it was not always so. In the early centuries after the death of Christ miracles were not seen in a particularly unusual light. In his book *The Decline and Fall of the Roman Empire*, Gibbon, who was no friend of Christianity, recorded that the setting aside of what appeared to be the law of nature was by no means unusual. The blind got their sight, the crippled walked, food was multiplied and the resurrection of the dead, was 'far from being an uncommon event'. I am not of course suggesting that a feed of pig's head and cabbage can be made to fly across the Burren at will. That would be a little hard on the intelligence as well as a bit unfair to the hoteliers. All I am asking is that we suspend judgment. After all a hundred years ago nobody believed you could fly to America in a few hours. When poor Marconi first mooted the idea of a wireless his friends put him in a mental home. It is of course doubtful if there is any such thing as a 'miracle'. Miracles seem to be no more than the working of the natural law at a level beyond our present understanding. As man evolves he will come to understand that law more and more.

If you cross the fields at Keelhilla to the ruins of St Colman MacDuagh's cave-church where they had the feed of pig's head and cabbage you can trace a little of Bother na Mias through the rocks. Nearby are some cursing stones but I won't advise you on them. However, do not forget to visit the grave of the poor simpleton – it is pin-pointed on the map – and say a prayer for the repose of his soul, just in case gluttony is regarded as a big sin in the next world. If you ever happen to be near Gort do call out to Kilmacduagh and see the remains of the beautiful cathedral built on the spot where St Colman got short-taken. There too you will see the leaning tower built by the drunken Connemara man. Why go to Pisa when we have one at home?

When you reach the main road at the village of Cappagh-more turn left and continue through Funshin More to the next crossroads. Turn left here over a Vee bend and you enter the Corker Pass. The old name for this was Corcair na gCléireach, or the Cells of the Clergy. Since this was the ancient highway from the outside world to Corcomroe Abbey it may well be that this was a halting place for the clergy where they could have a rest in some of the cells. Go through this picturesque valley and having travelled about two miles you will come to a little bohereen on your left near an elegant farm house, signposted Oughtmama. The Oughtmama churches are approximately a little over a mile along this bohereen. If the weather is fine you can bring your car safely about a half-a-mile along this track and walk the rest of the way. Here, in a delightfully sheltered spot hidden from the outside world are the remains of the three churches of Oughtmama. Oughtmama translated means the Breast of the Raised Pass and it is truly descriptive of this little paradise. Here we run into mystery again. Why three churches? Why not one only? Many theories are put forward but none are quite satisfactory.

Churches at Oughtmama

One theory says that the main church was for the public and the smaller ones for the monks. Another says that each church was built at a different time to commemorate a local martyr. Yet another says that wealthy families endowed and built the extra churches to commemorate their families and thereby ensure a place in heaven.

Again the smaller churches may well have been for private prayers or meditation – or indeed may have been Irish pyramids generating their own energy.

There was a belief that those buried within the precincts of a church or monastery ultimately got to heaven, which explains the presence of so many graves at such sites. Cynics, however, say that there was an added reason – a cash one. Monasteries charged a fee for burial, usually a horse, a cow, a chariot, a slave or some other workable commodity – and why should we blame them for taking advantage of a good opportunity and turning an honest penny – we all must live!

The truth is we really know very little about those far-off days. As yet we have been unable to get into the minds of those ancient Irish monks whose *Weltanschauung* we are still unable to understand.

A short distance to the north-east is a holy well dedicated to St Colman MacDuagh and a streamlet running out of it called Sruthán na Naomh – the Streamlet of the Saints. This well is reputed to have extraordinary medicinal properties. Apart from the usual one of curing warts it had special powers to cure sore eyes and even blindness 'for people have often washed their eyes in it which were veiled with thin film, and ere they had completed the third washing these films fell off leaving the eyes perfectly bright and clear-sighted.' Not far away one can find traces of an artificial water-channel which was used to turn an ancient mill-wheel to grind corn.

Here you have everything for a small community of monks, fertile land, fresh water, their own mill and enough churches to satisfy their prayerful needs. So sit down, take a rest, relax and go back in time to the seventh or eighth century when Oughtmama was a living, thriving community.

For me it has always been a kind of a little Shangri-La of the Burren. Everytime I come here I seem to lose contact with time and with the world outside and to be able to absorb myself in this shadow land of dreams, the undimmed beauty of our ancient past, that great and silent calm which none of us can reach. Sorry about all this but that is the effect those secret places of the Burren have on me.

> Most sweet it is with uplifted eyes
> To pace the ground, if path be there or none
> While a fair region round the traveller lies

Which he forbears again to look upon.
Pleased rather with some soft ideal scene
The work of fancy or some happy tone
Of meditation slipping in between
The beauty coming and the beauty gone.

When you get back to the road turn left and continue until you come to a T-junction. Turn right there and near Bell Harbour take another turn to the right for the ruins of the famous Abbey of Corcomroe. It was along this narrow lane in 1317 that a most bloody battle was fought between two Clare clans. Bloody battles were normal in those days but this one was unusual in that it was foretold by a banshee. She appeared to the army of Donogh O'Brien, one of the commanders, and the ancient scribe was not sparing in his vivid description:

It was a hag with a blue face, green teeth, rough hair, bent nails, lumpy forehead, eyes like red berries, large blue green nose, wide nostrils from which flowed a stream of snots, a turned up beard on her upper lip.

No wonder poor Donogh and his men were frightened. She warned them not to go to Corcomroe for 'though proud you march to the field of contest, soon shall ye perish with the exception of a very few. . . O fair Donogh you will not survive the fight.' She then mounted the wings of a huge raven and flew away. In case she would demoralise the army Donogh spoke to them:

Heed not the flowing predictions of this evil spirit who is endeavouring to strike dismay into your minds by pretending predictions of your death. Wherefore my nobles be not terrified but proceed on your journey with courage and valour to meet your enemies.

They proceeded as Donogh had urged them – but almost

everyone of them, including Donogh, was slain.

The old Irish kings were men of foresight and vision, if not exactly models of virtue. Donald O'Brien was one of these. As middle age began to recede he felt it would be prudent to keep a weather eye on the next world. A little insurance now might pay dividends later, and what better umbrella could he get under than to finance and build a monastery where the monks could pray for the happy repose of his soul in perpetuity. So he founded Corcomroe Abbey. According to the old scribes:

AD 1194 Donald O'Brien, King of Limerick founded a sumptuous monastery here for Cistercian monks and dedicated it to the Virgin Mary.

Church at Corcomroe, detail

The monastery was barely completed when Donald died – a compliment to his excellent sense of timing.

One of the most delightful things about Corcomroe is the name given to the monastery: *The Abbey of the Fertile Rock*. This name bespeaks for the whole burren. It is now known scientifically that rocks are not dead inanimate things. They are teeming with a thousand forms of life, not the least of which is the energy they store and give forth centuries later. The fertile rocks of Corcomroe, even today, give forth vibes of holiness and inspiration that were its past. If you doubt this just try it for yourself. Sit quietly in a corner of the Abbey or graveyard, close your eyes, relax your body completely, still the mind, stop thinking, and let impressions only come to you. Stay that way for ten or fifteen minutes and you will quickly realise that The Abbey of the Fertile Rock was truly a prophetic name.

Corcomroe was a different set-up entirely from Temple Cronan. It was a large Abbey ruled by an Abbot who had the same standing as a Bishop. In such Abbeys there were two kinds of monks, the ascetics and the manaigh. The ascetics were those who were fully professed and had taken the three vows. The manaigh were laymen who worked in and around the monastery at various jobs and who were only obliged to attend certain religious ceremonies. Many of them were married and lived with their families in the monastery grounds. They were however forbidden to have intercourse with their wives on Sundays, Wednesdays, Fridays and Saturdays. It was a strict rule that they were forbidden to have concubines. Can we assume from that rule that if they were not manaigh but ordinary lay-folk they could have concubines?

There seems, however, to have been an extrordinary liberalism in the air in those days. In the life of St Brendan of Clonfert there is an account of St Brendan chatting with his monks and telling them about a friend of his living near Corcomroe who was a man 'holy, blessed, perfect and righteous' – in other words a saint to be emulated. In a rather casual and matter-of-fact aside Brendan remarked that this saintly man 'had two excellent wives'. I leave that one to the theologians to sort out.

St Brendan seems to have been a helpful sort of fellow. A nun of St Ita's convent committed a little indiscretion with the gardener as a result of which she ran away to Connemara and gave birth there to a son. When St Brendan heard of her poverty and suffering he rescued her and brought her home to the convent where St Ita welcomed her and her child. Presumably the gardener was given other duties. Not all our saints were as Christlike as St Brendan and St Ita. Our 'glorious St Patrick' once drove his chariot three times over his own sister just because he caught her having a bit of a flutter with her lover. All the time while Patrick was foaming at the mouth and ranting with rage, the unfortunate woman, not thinking of herself, was praying for forgiveness for her lover. If ever I get to heaven I will be curious to find out which of the two got closest to the throne of God.

I have always had the gravest doubts whether or not St Patrick deserves the honoured place he holds in Irish history. The distinguished scholar, John Ryan S.J., wrote:

Patrick died in what was almost a blaze of glory and lived on in the popular memory as a great national figure, a worthy companion of heroes and kings.

This is pure nonsense. He was completely forgotten until the seventh century. They did not even know where he was buried nor do we know today. There is no reference to the shamrock in his life until the seventeenth century.

After the discovery of the manuscript of his *Confessions* he was resurrected in a propaganda exercise to promulgate the Roman dimension. He did not, in fact, bring Christianity to Ireland. A substantial part of the country had been Christianised before he came; but what he did do was to 'Romanise' the Celtic church and organise it into dioceses and parishes, obedient to Rome. The early Celtic church was very independent-minded and tended to pay scant attention to the Pope. Despite Patrick's hard work it took nearly seven centuries to finally bring the Celtic church into line. That happened in 1155 when Pope Adrian IV 'granted and donated Ireland' to the English King Henry II 'to be held by *him and his successors'*. Since then Rome has always recognised Britain's right to dominate and rule Ireland. Even the present Pope, John Paul II, publicly acknowledged that right when he recently appointed a Papal Nuncio to Britain with jurisdiction over the Six Counties and there was not even a whimper from our Department of Foreign Affairs.

Monks in those days lived by a rather strict rule but in Corcomroe they were lucky to be living under Cistercian rule. Had they been living under the savage unchristian rule of the Irish St Columbanus they would have good cause for complaint. Columbanus did not pull his punches:

He who when he gets a blessing and does not make the sign of the cross shall be punished with twelve strokes. He who eats without a blessing shall receive twelve strokes. He who does not control his cough in church shall receive six strokes. The priest who has not cut his finger nails before Mass, or the deacon who is not shaved shall receive six strokes.

There were also special canons known as 'equivalent' where the gentleman committing a misdemeanour had a choice:

1. The equivalent of a special fast: one hundred psalms and one hundred genuflections or one hundred and fifty-seven canticles.
2. The equivalent of one year: three days in the tomb of a dead saint without food, drink or sleep.
3. The equivalent of one year: forty days on bread and water, with a special fast each week. Forty psalms and sixty genuflections.

One or two others have always intrigued me. If you drank out of the same cup as a pregnant maid or the man living with her you could get forty lashes. And the same forty lashes if you sang the holy office after the death of a pregnant maid or the man living with her. It was absolutely imperative for a monk to be sober when singing his office. 'Anyone who is incapable of chanting the psalms owing to the thickness of his speech must fast for forty days.'

There was not, however, unanimous opinion on this matter. Maelruain of Tallaght told Dubithir of Finglas: 'Drink that causes forgetfulness of God shall not be drunk here.' Dubithir replied: 'I will allow my monks to drink and I bet they will be in heaven with yours.'

But Corcomroe, living under a wise Cistercian rule was spared this nonsense which many unfortunate Irishmen in other monasteries had to endure.

The Abbey lands must have comprised of at least two hundred acres. It had its farmyard, its horses, ploughs, dairy and barns. It would have a full complement too of blacksmiths, shoemakers, weavers, tailor, and all the other craftsmen to keep it going. But it seems as if one of the major roles of Corcomroe, situated as it was on a main highway, was that of catering for the many travellers, rich and poor who went that way. Inside the present gate there are the remains of what seems to have been part of the old guest house. The Cistercian rule provides that the monks must see the face of Christ in every traveller. I do admit that would stretch the imagination somewhat at the present day, but perhaps in those times it was not so difficult.

The traveller's meal would usually consist of two loaves of bread and slices of streaky bacon washed down by beer and honey. The meat would be flavoured by some kind of honey sauce. The ashes of burnt seaweed provided the salt. I once mused to myself about what would happen to me had I lived in the fourteenth century and turned up there one day as a weary traveller.

From the tower of the church they would have seen me coming in the far distance, together with Maxie, my staff and bag. The guestmaster would welcome me at the gate and bring me to the main guesthouse where there would be a warm fire heating stones for a Fualacht Fiadh where I could have a bath. Afterwards he would refresh me with some wine, victuals, bread and vegetables. While having the meal he would enquire about who I was, where I came from and where I was going. We would chat away then and I would tell him all the news I collected along my way. He in turn would appraise me and tell me what was happening in and around the Burren. He would then conduct me to my hut and show me my bed. Because all living things were seen as the reflection of God, he would bring me an armful of straw for Maxie to sleep on as well as providing a few succulent bones. He would then bring me for a visit to the church before turning in for the night. In the morning, after mass and breakfast, I would be brought to the Abbot himself and given his special blessing for a safe journey. If I had some money to pay them they would accept it. But if I had not no comment would be made.

Perhaps several travellers like that would visit Corcomroe daily. Some just passing through, others coming for a retreat, still others to study. All would be as welcome as

Christ.

Around the monastery one could meet quite a number of penitents doing some form of penance for their sinful deeds. The monasteries were accepted as places of sanctuary and immune from the law, so wanted men and women could find refuge there and could not be touched. What an interesting group of people to spend an evening with! As part of their atonement these penitents had to work hard, fast and pray. Because of this many left after a short interval. They found it more congenial to be on the run.

In the church itself there are many interesting things so well described in the guide books. One thing struck me however as delightful. Beside the carving of a smiling bishop, who looks as if he had dined well and there might be a thickening of speech, is a drawing of an oriental type boat. What seems to have happened was that some young apprentice did it while idling his lunch hour away when the Abbey was being built. He then quickly plastered over it before his master saw it. And hundreds of years later the plaster fell off and exposed the boat. But that is not all. On a visit to Corcomroe with a lady who is an expert on painted plasterwork in old churches she told me she had seen the exact same drawing in the Church of Hagia Sophia, in Trebizond, Turkey.

Not far from Corcomroe the O'Dalys ran their famous bardic school. It was a school of poetry and was in session from May to November mostly in the open air. One of the most famous of the O'Dalys was Cearbhaill who fell madly in love with a girl called Eileen, but she was betrothed to another man. On her wedding morning she eloped with Cearbhaill and they fled to Corcomroe in the hope of getting married there. The parents and their servants caught up with them before they got to the monastery and brought

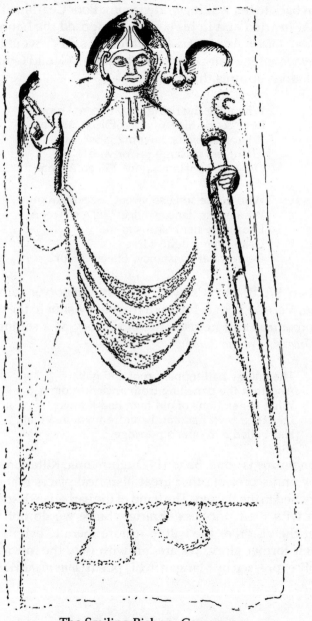

The Smiling Bishop, Corcomroe

Eileen back to her waiting bridegroom. Poor Cearbhaill was broken-hearted and in his sorrow composed the haunting melody, *Eileen Aroon* of which Mozart said 'I would die happy were I the composer of such music.' Gerald Griffin's translation captures the spirit:

> When like the rising day, Eileen Aroon
> Love sends his early ray, Eileen Aroon
> What makes his dawning glow
> Changless through joy or woe?
> Only the constant know, Eileen Aroon
>
> Who in the song so sweet? Eileen Aroon
> Who in the dance so fleet? Eileen Aroon
> Dear were her charms to me
> Dearer her laughter free
> Dearest her constancy, Eileen Aroon.

When W. B. Yeats stayed at Lady Gregory's summer house, Vernon Lodge, he was a frequent visitor to the ruins of Corcomroe and he used the old Abbey as a setting for *The Dreaming of the Bones*

> The enemy had toppled roof and gable
> And torn the panelling from ancient rooms,
> What generations of old men had known
> Like their own hand and children wondered at,
> Has boiled a trooper's porridge.

Corcomroe is gone. So too is Oughtmama, Kilfenora, Kilnaboy and scores of other great historical places that once flourished in the Burren. The hand of the barbarian destroyed them with their priceless libraries. Since we do not have either the vision or the will to restore them to even a part of their former glory, we are left with only the inevitable, so ably expressed by Mangan in his poem *Gone in the Wind*:

Solomon! Where is thy throne? It is gone in the wind.
Babylon! Where is thy might? It is gone in the wind.
Like the swift shadows of noon, like the dreams of the blind
Vanish the glories and pomps of the earth in the wind.

But the ivyed ruins live on as witnesses to the truth which
can never be destroyed. The words of Pádraig Pearse at the
grave of O'Donovan Rossa might well be their epitaph:
'The fools. The fools. They have left us our [Fenian] dead.'

EPILOGUE

Ill fares the land to hastening ills a prey
Where wealth accumulates and men
*   decay.*

OLIVER GOLDSMITH

Overlooking the square in the town of Arles in Provence, France, there is a prominent notice which reads:

TOURIST, you are in famous Provence, a country colonised, polluted and despoiled, its language forgotten, its ancient traditions betrayed, its soul extinguished.

This is an example of a town sick and tired of politicians, telling the truth about itself, No wonder it is thronged with tourists. Has the time now come to put up similar notices in Lisdoonvarna, Kilfenora and Ballyvaughan:

TOURIST, you are now in the famous Burren, a country polluted and despoiled, its language forgotten, its ancient traditions betrayed, its soul extinguished, the slow hand of death blighting its beauty and ravaging its historical heritage.

There are many concerned people who believe that the

Burren may well be on its way to becoming a wasteland – a real moonscape. The cause – air pollution, better known as acid rain. In other countries the effects of this type of pollution has been devastating. In Sweden 10,000 acres have been affected. Over half of West Germany's forests have been seriously damaged. Crop losses in the USA are now running at over three billion dollars every year. Most significant for the Burren is that ancient monuments in Greece disintegrated more in the past twenty years than they did in the preceding two thousand five hundred years.

Conservationists argue that the new ESB station at Moneypoint on the mouth of the Shannon may well be the culprit. They point out that in Germany, for example, the law forbids permits to be issued to power-stations capable of generating over 100 megawatts unless fitted with flue gas sulphur filters. Moneypoint, they say, has a capacity of over 900 megawatts and no adequate filters have been installed. Furthermore the conservationists state that this station will use over two million tons of coal every year which will release 75,000 tons of sulphur into the atmosphere and because of the prevailing south-westerly winds most of this is likely to fall on the Burren with disastrous results.

Understandably the ESB deny this. They say that they have taken adequate precautions to ensure clean air and in addition they have erected a number of monitoring stations, including one in the Burren, to test the air. The arguments for and against are very technical and unlikely to be understood by the average layman. Nevertheless if there is even a shadow of doubt it would be prudent for responsible local groups to monitor the air also, and to be given access to all available data at the station itself as well as the right to inspect it. One cannot be too careful with the environment. Most European countries are now realising, alas too late, that their past negligence is having devastating results. The old proverb 'Eternal vigilance is the price of freedom' is fully applicable here. Some time ago Prince Bernhard of the Netherlands was moved to say:

We are poisoning the air over our cities, we are poisoning the rivers and the seas, we are poisoning the soil itself. . . if we don't get together in a real and mighty effort to stop these attacks on Mother Earth, we may find ourselves one day – one day soon maybe – in a world that will be only a desert full of plastic, concrete and electronic robots. In that world there will be no more 'nature', in that world man and a few domestic animals will be the only living creatures. Yet man cannot live without some measure of contact with nature. It is essential to his happiness.

But perhaps the most inspiring words of all were spoken more than one hundred and fifty years ago by the Indian Chief Seattle – words which make a suitable ending to this book. The President of the United States of America offered to buy the Indian lands and look after the tribes in a reservation. Chief Seattle replied as follows:

To the Great White Chief,
Washington.

Greetings!
The Great White Chief sends word that he wishes to buy our land, and reserve a place for us so that we can live comfortably to ourselves. We will consider your offer to buy our land but it will not be easy.

How can you buy or sell the sky, the warmth of the land? If we do not own the freshness of the air, and the sparkle of the water, how can you buy them? Every part of this earth is sacred to my people. Every shining pine needle, every sandy shore, every mist in the dark woods, every small and humming insect is holy in the memory and experience of my people. We are part of the earth and it is part of us. The perfumed flowers are our sisters, the deer, the horse, the great eagle, these are our brothers. All belong to the same family.

This shining water that moves in the streams and rivers is not just water but the blood of our ancestors. If we sell you land, you must remember that it is sacred and you must teach your children that it is sacred and that each ghostly reflection in the clear water of the lakes tells of events and memories in the life of my people. The waters murmur in the voice of my father's father.

We know that the white man does not understand our ways. One portion of the land is the same to him as another for he is a stranger who comes in the night and takes from the land whatever he needs. The earth is not his brother, but his enemy, and when he has used it he moves on. He treats his mother the earth and his brother, the sky, as things to be bought, plundered and sold like bright beads. His appetite will devour the earth and leave behind only a desert.

Our ways are different from your ways. The sight of your cities pains the eyes of the red man. But perhaps it is because the red man is a savage and does not understand. There is no quiet place in the white man's cities. No place to hear the unfurling of leaves in spring, or the rustle of the insect wings. The clatter only seems to insult the ears. And what is there to live for if a man cannot hear the lonely cry of the frogs around a pond at night. The red man prefers the soft sound of the wind darting over the face of the waters, and the smell of the wind itself, cleansed by a mid-day rain or scented with the tall pine.

The air is precious to the red man for all things share the same breath. The white man does not seem to notice the air he breathes. Like a man dying for many days he is numb to the stench. I am a savage and I do not understand any other way.

I have seen a thousand rotting buffalos on the prairie left by the white man who shot them from a passing train. I do not understand how the smoking iron horse can be more important than the buffalo that we kill only to live. What is a man without the beasts? If all the beasts were gone, man would die from a great loneliness of spirit. For whatever happens to the beasts happens to man.

This we know: the earth does not belong to man; man belongs to the earth. Whatever befalls the earth befalls the sons of earth.

Man did not weave the web of life, he is merely a strand in it. This earth is precious to God and to harm the earth is to heap contempt on its Creator. The whites too shall pass. Contaminate your bed and you will one night suffocate in your own waste. Where is the thicket? Gone. Where is the eagle? Gone. The end of living and the beginning of survival has come.

Chief Seattle and his tribe lost out to the white man and today their beautiful lands, once alive to the throb of living things are savaged, wasted and withered. Will this fate overtake the Burren? When? Five years? Ten years? Twenty years? Or sooner?